GAIL GRECO'S
LITTLE
Bed & Breakfast
COOKBOOK SERIES

Recipes for Romance

Text by GAIL GRECO

Photographs by TOM BAGLEY

RUTLEDGE HILL PRESS®
Nashville, Tennessee
A Thomas Nelson Company

Published by Rutledge Hill Press, a Thomas Nelson Company, P. O. Box 141000, Nashville, Tennessee 37214.

Photographs by Tom Bagley

Photo art direction and styling by Gail Greco

Food preparation assistance by Priscilla Powers, Mary Lynn Tucker, and Yvonne Martin

Editorial assistance by Tricia Conaty

Photo on page 92 courtesy of Woods House

Cover and book design by Gore Studio, Inc.

Text layout and typesetting by John Wilson Design

All recipes selected and edited for the home kitchen by Gail Greco

ON THE FRONT COVER: CHICKEN CHEVRE PATISSERIE AT SQUIRE TARBOX INN, WISCASSET, MAINE. RECIPE ON PAGE 39.

PHOTO OPPOSITE TITLE PAGE: THE LOBSTER STEW, RECIPE ON PAGE 8

Greco, Gail.
        Recipes for romance / Gail Greco ; photography by Tom Bagley.
                p. cm.
        Includes index.
        ISBN 1-55853-455-5
        1. Cookery for two.   I. Title.
    TX652.G728   1996
    641.5'61—dc20   96-30489
                                            CIP

Printed in the United States of America

2 3 4 5 6 7 8 9 — 05 04 03 02 01 00

THE INN AT CEDAR FALLS, LOGAN, OHIO

For Tom,
for sharing with me the romance that is
love, art, poetry, music, creativity,
and, most importantly, our
own memorable meals together.

Contents

Rosemary and Apple-Cider-Glazed
"Love" Hens

Elderberry and Ginger Duckling

DESSERT
47

Strawberry Shortbread Shortcakes

Iced Mocha Cappuccino Cheesecake

Chocolate Hazelnut Torte

Sweet Chèvre Pound Cake

Chocolate Raisin Pie

Coconut Coffee Ice Cream Pie with Oreo
Crust and Amaretto-Chocolate Sauce

Baked Orange-Almond Custard

Hot Fudge-and-Peanut-Butter
Banana Split

THE MORNING AFTER
65

Vanilla Varoom Through a Straw

Panama Canal in a Glass

Plums in Port Wine Sauce

Peaches-'n'-Cream-Cheese Bread Pudding
with Raspberry Sauce

Blueberry Cottage Pudding

Apple Pie Pizza with Cheddar-Cheese Crust

Homemade Maple-and-Nut Granola

Cinnamon Rolls with "Royal" Icing

Popovers with Lemon Curd

Sausage-and-Cheese Breakfast Scones

One-Dish Breakfast Risotto

Baked Crêpe Cups Lorraine

Tomato-and-Egg Pesto in Puff Pastry

Tomato-Polenta Torte

Lobster Breakfast Pie

Puff Pear Pancake

Gingerbread-Raisin Pancakes with
Lemon Sauce

Carrot Pecan Pancakes

Nutty Cheese-and-Apricot-Stuffed French
Toast with Gingered-Peach Syrup

Other Books in This Series

∾∘∾

The Test Kitchen for the
Cooking Association of Country Inns

Although all inn recipes are tried-and-true and served at the inns all the time, the recipes in this cookbook have been further verified and tested for accuracy and clarification for the home kitchen.

The cooking seal of approval that accompanies this book, means that every recipe has been tested in kitchens other than the source, and that the association test kitchen has been satisfied that the recipe is proven and worthy of preparing.

The test kitchen is under the leadership of association founder Gail Greco, with Charla Honea and other editors at Rutledge Hill Press assisting. The prestigious list of kitchen testers is as follows:

∞○∞

DAVID CAMPICHE, *Chef/Owner*
The Shelburne Inn • Seaview, Washington

YVONNE MARTIN, *Chef/Owner*
The White Oak Inn • Danville, Ohio

DEBBIE MOSSIMAN, *Chef/Owner*
Swiss Woods • Lititz, Pennsylvania

PATRICK RUNKEL, *Chef/Owner*
October Country Inn • Bridgewater Corners, Vermont

LAURA SIMOES, *Chef/Owner*
The Inn at Maplewood Farm • Hillsborough, New Hampshire

ELIZABETH TURNEY, *Chef/Owner*
Bear Creek Lodge • Victor, Montana

MARION YADON, *Chef/Owner*
Canyon Villa Bed & Breakfast • Sedona, Arizona

Cuisine that Charms

I WONDER: WHEN YOU picked up this book, did you immediately think of it as a book to inspire romance at the table with someone you love or dream about? If you did, you were correct. Romance is certainly about the desires, hopes, dreams, and plans for absorbing life's precious moments with a significant other, but it is also about a whole lot more.

Romance. Even the word sounds rapturous—sumptuous. That is because romance is something all-encompassing—a total celebration of the senses. Romance is something that occurs when you encounter lovely visions, memorable reverberations, intoxicating scents, new and unusual textures to explore, and, of course, indescribable tastes.

Anyone can find romance as long as he or she appeals to the five senses by using them imaginatively. When you put poetry and art in everything you see, hear, feel, smell, and taste, this intangible thing called romance will find you—especially in the kitchen and at the table. Romance is about taking advantage of your own good fortune as a sensuous being, and this book is about how the pleasures of the kitchen have a great deal to do with all of that.

We have to be constantly reminded of the small things that offer us our greatest happiness. Not long ago, the term comfort food was applied to down-home traditional recipes that were making a comeback in the stress-filled nineties. Imagine food offering you a *comforting* moment? Well, why not? Food is *affective*. It can offer an

PEARS ARE ROMANTIC WHETHER IN THE MORNING ON THE TILED PORCH AT BECKMANN INN OR AS A SNACK IN THE AFTERNOON WHILE THE SUN SPARKLES ON THE WATER LIKE CRYSTAL AT LODGE ON LAKE LURE.

[*xi*]

exhilarating experience. Romantic recipes are blueprints that excite the senses, cuisine that charms and complements the ambiance you have created for yourself and someone else at the table.

The environment at bed-and-breakfasts and country inns is one of our greatest sources of romance. Right now I'm sitting in front of a blazing fire with the soft strains of a harp playing in the background, and there's candlelight on the table. Innkeeper Karen Mitman is in the barn feeding newborn Nubian goats.

This is just breakfast time at the Squire Tarbox, one small inn, filling its guests with romance.

Innkeepers know how to stimulate all of our senses, right down to the smallest details. The Elk Cove Inn in Elk, California, exemplifies that point literally when it advertises that sheets and towels at their place are "sun-dried." You form a picture in your mind of slipping into inviting bedding that smells and feels good as well as looks good. Romance has begun.

From the decor to the gardens and the service, and most of all the food, inns are so attractive to us because they are romantic. Food is an important element of inn-going. Inns are my favorite places to dine when not at home. They offer quiet moments at a table where I can really taste and smell the food and where the ingredients are the freshest. With *Recipes for Romance* in hand, you can foster romance and even put love on a plate with recipes that get the juices flowing in more ways than one. I know that *Recipes for Romance* is a cliche but when it comes to bed-and-breakfasts and country inns, there is no better way to say it.

In this book, the chapter called *Flirtations* explores starters such as soups and appetizers that tease before more culinary pleasures come along. *The Main Course* includes entrée choices, some a bit fancier than others, depending on how dressy or casual a dinner you are planning. *Dessert* wraps up a sensuous meal with sweet indulgences that will ensure a memorable experience. I also traveled the country for *The Morning After* section, seeking a variety that served up luxurious selections for lingering. It would be my own pleasure if you could keep the notion of romance in your head and your heart all day by giving yourself a good start at a candlelit breakfast table, with a breakfast tray in

bed, or with an eye-opening morning on a patio.

People spend hundreds of dollars seeking the quiet, personal pleasures afforded by such stress deflectors as health spas and aromatherapy. Can you think of any better aromatherapy to make you feel good all over than food cooking or baking in your kitchen? A survey done by the Smell and Taste Treatment and Research Foundation in Chicago measured the blood flow of young male students and found it was the scent of cinnamon buns that turned them on. I wouldn't dream of completing this book without including a cinnamon rolls recipe, and along with it, other recipes that will keep you turned on to life and all its endless possibilities for romance.

Flirtations

Wild 'n' Warm Watercress Soup

Watercress grows near streams and brooks. But let me introduce you to this recipe with the gentle words of its creator, innkeeper Neil Myers, who walks the grounds of the inn to pick bouquets of watercress: "We serve this soup fall, winter, and spring before the watercress bolts [flowers] in the warm weather. We gather the watercress from our spring which feeds the very clean, cold water it needs to flourish." Neil notes that the homemade chicken stock is essential, because of the delicate flavoring of the soup.

Chapter Opener: A room in the barn, and Asparagus Goat Cheese strudels at Squire Tarbox Inn, recipe on page 20

Left: Vaucluse Spring innkeeper Neil Myers, gathering watercress

[3]

Wild 'n' Warm Watercress Soup (continued)

2	large bouquets watercress (2 generous cups), plus 6 sprigs for garnish
1/4	cup (1/2 stick) plus 1 table-spoon butter
3	cups homemade chicken stock
1	medium onion, chopped
1/2	stalk celery, thinly sliced
1 1/2	leeks, white part only, finely chopped

1/4	cup all-purpose flour
2	cups half-and-half
	Salt and white pepper
	Lemon juice, sherry, or brandy, optional
	Sour cream for garnish

MAKES 6 SERVINGS

Pick off enough watercress leaves to fill 1 cup. Heat 1 tablespoon of the butter in a medium saucepan and simmer the watercress leaves with 1/4 cup of the chicken stock for about 5 minutes or until wilted. Pour the mixture through a strainer, reserving the stock and the leaves separately. Set aside.

Coarsely chop the remaining watercress and stems. Add 1 more tablespoon of butter and 1/2 cup of the stock to the reserved butter/stock mixture. Heat over medium heat. When hot, add the onions, celery, leeks, and chopped watercress.

Turn the heat down and simmer for 10 minutes.

In a medium saucepan, heat the remaining butter with the flour until combined. Add the onion and watercress mixture and stir. Add the remaining stock and half-and-half, stirring constantly. Turn heat down to a simmer and cook for 10 minutes.

Pour the soup through a strainer and add the reserved watercress leaves. Season with salt and pepper. Taste the soup and add a squeeze of lemon, or sherry, or brandy, if desired. Serve hot, garnished with a dollop of sour cream and a sprig of cress.

THE INN AT VAUCLUSE SPRING

Curried Broccoli Soup

∾౦∾

The name of this recipe tells only half of the story. Broccoli predominates but there is a host of other vegetables in this bowl of hearty cold-weather fare. The curry awakens the taste buds and coaxes the stubborn into open-mindedness .

The glowing carriage lamp beside the door of a country inn, when viewed through a cold rain, erases the rigors of the day and promises a fine, fine evening.
—Elizabeth Squier, Country Inns of New England

2	heads broccoli (1 to 1 ½ pounds)		2	quarts chicken stock
2	tablespoons butter		½	cup lemon juice
2	tablespoons olive oil		2	ripe Roma tomatoes
1	large onion, thinly sliced		¼	cup chopped Italian parsley
6	cloves garlic, finely chopped		½	pound spinach
2	leeks (white with some green), finely diced			Salt and pepper
1	carrot, finely diced		2	tablespoons honey
3	tablespoons uncooked white rice			Chopped parsley for garnish
2	teaspoons curry powder			Plain yogurt for garnish

MAKES 8 TO 10 SERVINGS

Discard the tough bottoms from the broccoli. Peel the stems and dice finely. Coarsely dice the broccoli florets. In a large stockpot, heat the butter and oil and sauté the onion, garlic, leeks, carrot, and rice, stirring until the vegetables are wilted (do not

brown). Add the curry, stock, lemon juice, broccoli, tomatoes, and parsley. Bring the mixture to a boil, then reduce to low heat and simmer for 30 minutes. Add the spinach. Season with salt and pepper. Add the honey. Cook until the spinach is wilted, about 1 minute. Ladle into the bowls and sprinkle with parsley and a swirl of yogurt, if desired.

SIGNING THE GUESTBOOK AT THE KING'S COTTAGE

BEAR CREEK LODGE

Sherried Lobster Stew

Lobster and a charming room for the night are the amenities that bring guests to this seacoast inn in one of the most romantic harbor villages anywhere. Be sure to try Cappy's Bakery—you might as well be in Provence. The chef at Blue Harbor House makes this stew with the lobster shells to add flavor. I have left them out of this recipe to simplify it, but add them to the stew during the 1 ½ hours simmering time, if you desire, and discard before serving.

THE STEW AT CAMDEN HARBOR

2	cups water	1	small can (3- to 4-ounces) evaporated milk
4	medium red potatoes, peeled		
6	teaspoons butter	2	cups whole milk
1/2	cup medium-diced onion	1	cup dry cooking sherry
1/2	cup medium-diced celery	2	cups lobster meat
1/2	cup grated carrots	1	teaspoon sesame seeds
1/4	cup finely chopped scallions		Salt and pepper
1/4	cup small-diced leeks		Fresh parsley sprigs for garnish
1/4	cup small-diced red bell pepper		
1/4	cup small-diced green bell pepper		

MAKES 6 TO 8 SERVINGS

*F*ill *a saucepan with the water. Add the potatoes and bring to a boil. Cook for about 20 minutes or until tender. Drain, but reserve the liquid. Cut the potatoes into quarters. Set aside.*

In a large non-reactive stockpot, melt 4 teaspoons of the butter over medium-high heat. Add the onions, celery, carrots, scallions, leeks, and bell peppers. Sauté until the vegetables are just tender. Add both milks, sherry, cooked potatoes, and reserved potato water. Lower the heat and simmer for 10 minutes.

Meanwhile, melt the remaining 2 teaspoons of butter in a large skillet. Toss the lobster meat into the skillet along with the sesame seeds. Sauté for about 5 minutes and then transfer to the stew ingredients simmering in the stockpot. Continue cooking the stew over low heat for 1 1/2 hours. Season with salt and pepper. Garnish with parsley.

BLUE HARBOR HOUSE

Baby Romaine Salad with Warmed Sundried Pepper Vinaigrette

卍

Michael Sheehan, chef and innkeeper at Prospect Hill, has a light, gentle, but intense touch when it comes to cooking. This inviting salad not only complements the innkeeper's warm hospitality, but also reflects the personality of this inn, one of my long-time favorites. Jicama is a root vegetable with the taste of water chestnuts and is a good source of vitamin C and potassium. Peel the vegetable and cut julienne-style. Sundried tomatoes may be substituted for the sundried bell peppers.

Dressing		*Assembly*	
1/2	cup chopped sundried bell peppers	4	heads baby Romaine lettuce, separated
1/3	cup port wine	1/2	cup julienne - cut jicama, for garnish
1/3	cup balsamic vinegar		Freshly cracked pepper
2/3	cup extra-virgin olive oil		
1	teaspoon minced garlic		
1/3	cup chopped fresh basil		

MAKES 4 SERVINGS

*M*arinate the dried peppers in the port for at least half an hour at room temperature. In a mixing bowl, combine the rest of the ingredients, stirring well. Add the peppers with the port and let stand a few minutes. Stir the mixture well and warm a few seconds in a small saucepan, just to take any chill off the dressing. Wash and divide the lettuce among four serving plates. Drape the warm dressing over the lettuce and add the jicama and a few twists of freshly cracked pepper. Serve immediately.

PROSPECT HILL

Grilled Portobello Mushrooms with a Florentine Topping

ᔇᐤᔄ

Portobello mushrooms are meaty and versatile. This version is simple and impressive. The inn also garnishes the plate with half of a grilled zucchini.

Mushrooms

1/2	cup olive oil
1/4	cup balsamic vinegar
1	garlic clove, finely minced
	Salt and freshly cracked pepper
4	medium-sized portobello mushrooms, stems reserved and cut into 1/2-inch pieces

Topping

1/2	cup olive oil
1/2	medium red onion
2	scallions, cut into 1/4-inch pieces
1	garlic clove, minced
2	cups fresh spinach leaves, shredded
2	Roma tomatoes, seeded and cut into a small dice
1	tablespoon finely diced fresh basil
1/4	cup balsamic vinegar
	Salt and freshly cracked pepper
	Fresh chopped herbs for garnish
	Crème fraîche for garnish

MAKES 4 SERVINGS

In a small mixing bowl, mix together the oil, vinegar, and garlic. Season with salt and pepper. Place the mushroom caps in a small baking dish and pour the marinade over them, coating the mushrooms well. Grill the mushroom caps until browned, basting with any excess marinade.

Meanwhile, prepare the topping. In a medium skillet, over medium-high heat, heat the olive oil and sauté the onions, reserved mushroom stems, scallions, and garlic until tender. Add the spinach and tomatoes. Stir and add the basil and vinegar. Heat for a few seconds more and season with salt and pepper.

Place a mushroom cap in the center of a plate and add the topping, draping some of it over the sides of the mushroom cap. Garnish with herbs and crème fraîche, if desired.

TRANQUIL HOUSE

Salmon and Onion Cheesecake

୨~ଡ୧

People in the Pacific Northwest think seafood all the time. This clever rendition has all of the makings of a star on dinner tables across the country. The texture is sumptuous as is the tasteful pairing of the Blue cheese with the salmon. Our testers preferred a quality Danish Blue cheese that is creamy and flavorful. This also makes a wonderful entrée for a light supper with bread and salad.

When giving a dinner party, always give a short narration as to what is in the food. Give a tour of the ingredients. This activity gets mouths watering and offers a better appreciation of the food you have so thoughtfully prepared.

¹/₂	cup, plus 3 tablespoons grated Parmesan cheese	¹/₂	cup finely chopped onion
¹/₃	cup fine unseasoned breadcrumbs	¹/₂	cup small-diced red bell pepper
		5	ounces smoked salmon, cut into small pieces

Filling

3 ¹/₂	(8-ounce) packages cream cheese, at room temperature	¹/₂	cup blue cheese
4	eggs	2	tablespoons chopped fresh tarragon
¹/₃	cup heavy cream		Salt and freshly cracked pepper
3	tablespoons butter		

MAKES 10 SERVINGS

*P*reheat the oven to 300°. Sprinkle ¹/₂ cup of the Parmesan cheese and the bread-crumbs partly up the sides and evenly over the bottom of a lightly greased 10-inch springform pan. Shake and turn the pan until all surfaces are completely coated. In the large bowl of an electric mixer, combine the cream cheese, eggs, and heavy cream, beating until thoroughly blended and smooth.

Melt the butter in a medium skillet set on medium–high heat. Add the onions and red peppers. Sauté for a few minutes, until the onions are translucent. Gently fold the vegetables into the cream cheese mixture, followed by the smoked salmon, blue cheese, the remaining 3 tablespoons of Parmesan, and the tarragon. Stir carefully until all the ingredients are combined. Season with salt and pepper.

Pour the batter into the prepared pan. Gently shake the contents to level the mixture. Cover the pan with aluminum foil from the bottom up around the sides only to keep any water from seeping into the cheesecake as you set it in a larger pan filled with about 2 inches of water. Do not allow the edges of the pans to come in contact with each other.

Bake for 1 hour and 40 minutes or until golden, then turn off the heat and allow the cake to sit in the oven for an additional hour. Lift the cheesecake out of the water bath and cool on a rack for at least 2 hours before unmolding. Slice and serve either at room temperature or cold.

CAPTAIN WHIDBEY INN

[13]

Baked Tomato-and-Cheese Tart

✍︎

Although the recipe calls for a pre-made pie crust, you may opt to use a crust of your own. Use a quality fresh mozzarella here. It really does make a difference.

½	of a (15-ounce) package of refrigerated pie crust	3	medium-size ripe tomatoes, blanched, peeled, and cut into ½-inch slices
2	cups (8 ounces) coarsely grated Mozzarella cheese	1 ½	tablespoons extra-virgin olive oil
¼	cup minced fresh basil		Salt and freshly cracked pepper
1	tablespoon freshly chopped oregano or ½ tablespoon dried		

MAKES 8 SERVINGS

*P*reheat the oven to 400°. Roll the pie crust to pie-plate shape, about ¼-inch thick. Place the pie crust in a 10-inch tart pan, or quiche dish that has been very lightly coated with cooking oil spray. Trim any excess pastry. Generously prick the bottom

and sides of the dough. Bake for 5 minutes, just to turn the dough a bit crusty. Sprinkle the cheese over the bottom of the crust and follow with half of the basil and all of the oregano. Arrange the tomato slices on the crust. Brush with the olive oil and season with salt and pepper. Place the tart on a baking sheet and bake on the lower rack 35 to 40 minutes or until tomatoes are cooked. Remove from the oven and sprinkle with the remaining basil.

GAIL'S KITCHEN

[15]

Artichoke and Roasted Garlic French Bread

∽ం∾

MORNING BREADS AT FAIRVILLE INN IN PENNSYLVANIA

Serving crusty bread is romantic. Brother Peter Reinhart of *Brother Juniper's Bread Book* puts it this way, "The intoxicating aroma of fresh baked bread can chase the blues away . . . transcending the senses through which it reaches us, it lifts our spirit toward the good, the hopeful, and the ideal."

Innkeeper Elizabeth Turney makes some of the best I have ever tasted. This recipe can include fillings such as sun-dried tomatoes with sausage or Kalamata olives with Feta cheese or simply plain. You decide. Like any important friendship, this bread takes nurturing but it is not time consuming. Elizabeth recommends using a pizza stone for added crustiness. You will need 16x4-inch French bread-baking pans.

Night before		4 to 5	cups unbleached all-purpose flour
1	tablespoon sugar		
1	cup warm water	1	cup chopped marinated artichoke hearts, squeezed dry
1	package active dry yeast		
2	cups unbleached all-purpose flour	1	whole bulb roasted garlic, finely minced
			Cornmeal for sprinkling
Next morning			Olive oil
2	cups warm water		Water in an atomizer
2	teaspoons salt		
1/2	cup whole wheat flour		

MAKES 2 LOAVES

*B*egin making the bread by preparing the starter the night before serving. Combine the sugar and water in a large bowl. Sprinkle with the yeast and stir gently. Slowly stir the flour in with a fork until smooth. Place the yeast mixture in a tightly covered container and refrigerate overnight.

Next morning, remove the starter and place in a food processor fitted with a dough hook or paddle. Turn the processor to low and add the 2 cups of warm water and then the salt. Begin beating in both flours, a little at a time. (Stop adding flour when dough is sticky.) Continue beating on low for about 5 minutes. Place in an oiled bowl. Cover and refrigerate for 6 to 8 hours.

Preheat the oven to 450°. Remove the dough from the refrigerator and punch down. Cut in half and shape into 2 rectangles, a little shorter than the pans and about half as wide. Spread the artichoke hearts and garlic on the dough, fold sides up, over-lapping on top. Seal the ends. Put the pizza stone in the oven (if using one). Oil the two troughs of the French-bread pan and sprinkle with cornmeal. Place the dough in the pan and let sit at room temperature, covered with a towel, for 45 to 60 minutes or until the dough reaches the top of the troughs. Slash the top diagonally with a knife 3 to 4 times. Spray lightly with water and place in the oven on a pizza stone.

Place a few ice cubes in the bottom of the oven for more moisture. Turn oven down to 400° and bake for 40 to 50 minutes. After 20 minutes, spray the dough again. Bread is done when it sounds hollow when tapped.

BEAR CREEK LODGE

[17]

Sausage-and-Mushroom Stuffed Pillows

〜o〜

When making small appetizers, I find it best to make a large batch and freeze, taking out as needed. This recipe comes from a precious little inn with romantic, period guest rooms.

THE INN AT OLDE NEW BERLIN IN PENNSYLVANIA

	Olive oil for sautéing	1/4	teaspoon salt
1/4	cup finely diced onions	1/2	cup Asiago cheese
1/4	cup finely diced mushrooms	1/3	cup seasoned breadcrumbs
1	pound ground Italian sweet sausage	1/4	pound phyllo dough
1/8	teaspoon cayenne pepper		Egg wash
1/8	teaspoon white pepper		

MAKES 48 PILLOWS

*P*reheat the oven to 350°. In a large skillet, heat the olive oil over medium-high heat. Sauté the onions and mushrooms until crisp tender. Add the sausage and continue to cook for a few minutes or until the sausage is browned. Season with the peppers and the salt. Remove the pan from the heat. Stir in the Asiago and breadcrumbs. Set aside.

Carefully separate the sheets of phyllo dough and arrange them on a flat surface. Cut the sheets into 3x10-inch strips. Place about 1/2 ounce of the sausage mixture 1 inch from the top of each phyllo rectangle. Roll the strips at alternate angles around the filling, forming closed triangles. (See photo on page 44.) Place the phyllo pillows on a baking sheet and brush with egg wash. Bake for 5 to 10 minutes or until golden brown.

THE INN AT OLDE NEW BERLIN

THE INN'S RESTAURANT TAKES ITS NAME FROM THE ANGEL GABRIEL

Asparagus and Goat Cheese Strudels

✧

Dining at the Squire Tarbox is casual but elegant and so romantic. The flickering candlelight highlights the warmth of the walls, floors, and ceiling, all of which were made from original pumpkin pine woods. If you cannot find garlic-and-chive goat cheese, write to the inn, which ships the cheese out by mail order. Our testers made this dish without the ham and found equally exciting results. You may add a pool of red bell pepper purée.

Start a kitchen journal for happy thoughts from kitchen to table. Everything is "fare" game for the journal. One day I was in a coffee shop and became fascinated by a gadget for grating the nutmeg over a cup of coffee. I wrote about it in my kitchen journal. You will be surprised how fast the journal fills up!

32	thin asparagus, woody ends snapped and discarded	16	sheets phyllo dough, thawed
8	ounces garlic-and-chive goat cheese	4	tablespoons unsalted butter, melted
1	egg	8	$1/16$-inch thick slices prosciutto or baked ham
$1/8$	teaspoon salt		Fresh dill for garnish
$1/8$	teaspoon freshly cracked pepper		

MAKES 8 SERVINGS

Cook the asparagus in gently boiling salted water just until tender, about 2 to 3 minutes. Drain and rinse in cold water to stop the cooking process.

In a mixing bowl, combine the cheese, egg, salt, and pepper. Set aside.

Preheat the oven to 400°. Unwrap the phyllo dough and cover with a clean, damp kitchen towel. Carefully lift up 2 sheets of phyllo together and fold in half. (Use 2 sheets per appetizer.) Arrange the dough lengthwise on a flat surface. Brush gently with melted butter until saturated.

Place 1 slice of prosciutto on the buttered dough about 2 inches from the top. Spread 1 rounded tablespoon of the cheese mixture on the prosciutto. Then arrange 3 tips of asparagus over the cheese to complete the filling. Roll the phyllo dough over the filling 2 more times. Brush with butter. Fold in the sides, brush with butter, and continue rolling to the end of the dough. Brush the seam and the top of the bundle with butter, and place on a mesh wire rack, seam side down. Continue assembling until all of the strudels are formed.

When all the appetizers are prepared, place the mesh wire rack on a foil-lined cookie sheet. Bake the strudels for 10 to 15 minutes or until golden brown and heated through. To serve, slice the strudel on the diagonal and arrange on individual plates. Garnish with the herb of your choice and an asparagus tip for each strudel.

THE SQUIRE TARBOX INN

The Main Course

Bow-Tie Pasta with Tomato Porcini Sauce

༄o

The sauce is so delightful and full-bodied that it can be served with a number of different pasta shapes. I like the bow-ties because they are artful and really hold the sauce. The recipe calls for pancetta, an Italian bacon, but you may substitute regular bacon. The sauce yields 4 cups so that you can serve fewer people, boil less pasta, and freeze the remaining sauce.

I called a friend on her birthday. She was baking her own cake, just in case someone forgot what day it was. "I'm tired of shying away from birthdays. It is my birthday, and I'm going to celebrate it whether anyone else does or doesn't. This is my life," she said. I found the notion most uplifting.

CHAPTER OPENER: CHICKEN CHÈVRE PÂTISSERIE AT SQUIRE TARBOX INN, RECIPE ON PAGE 39

Sauce

1 to 2	ounces dried porcini mushrooms
1	cup hot water
1	tablespoon olive oil
2	ounces pancetta
1	medium onion, cut into a small dice
2	teaspoons minced fresh rosemary (1 teaspoon dried), plus 4 sprigs for garnish
1/8	teaspoon Italian red pepper flakes
1	28-ounce can crushed Italian tomatoes with added purée
1	teaspoon sugar
	Salt and freshly cracked pepper

Pasta

1 1/2	pounds farfalle (bow-tie pasta)
	Grated Asiago or Parmesan cheese
1/2	pound Ricotta cheese

MAKES 4 SERVINGS

*R*inse the mushrooms under cold water and soak them in a small bowl with the hot water for about 30 minutes or until softened. Drain and reserve the soaking water. In a medium saucepan, add the olive oil and sauté the pancetta over medium heat

for 2 minutes. Add the onion and rosemary and cook until the onion is translucent, stirring occasionally with a wooden spoon for about 8 minutes. Stir in the red pepper flakes. Add the tomatoes and mushrooms and pour in the reserved mushroom liquid through a fine-mesh strainer. Stir in the sugar. Simmer the sauce until thickened, about 35 minutes. Season with salt and pepper.

While the sauce cooks, bring a large pot of water to a boil. Cook the pasta until al dente. Strain and serve with the sauce. Sprinkle with grated cheese. Garnish with a dollop of Ricotta on top of the pasta and add a sprig of fresh rosemary.

Glazed Pork Tenderloin Al Fresco with Citrus-Fennel Sauce

⚬⚬⚬

Blanketed in a honey-lime cilantro glaze, this moist dish makes a delightful meal accompanied by a mixed grains-and-rice or angel-hair pasta. Slice the pork into medallions and place over the grains or pasta. The tenderloin soaks in spicy-fennel brine for 2 days before cooking.

When sleeping in someone else's home or at an inn, do not place a suitcase or anything else on top of the bed. Beds deserve more respect than that. Don't even sit on the bed unless the cover has been turned down.

Pork		Glaze	
2	quarts water	$^1/_4$	cup ($^1/_2$ stick) butter
$^2/_3$	cup sugar	1	tablespoon minced fresh fennel
$^1/_3$	cup salt	$^1/_2$	cup pure honey
2	tablespoons minced fresh fennel or 1 tablespoon dried	2 $^1/_2$	tablespoons fresh lime juice
		1	teaspoon cornstarch
2	tablespoons crushed dry fennel seed	1	tablespoon chopped fresh cilantro
2	tablespoons dried thyme leaves	1	teaspoon grated lime peel
		1	teaspoon grated orange peel
2	tablespoons freshly cracked pepper	$^1/_8$	teaspoon dried ground fennel
	grated peel from 1 large orange	$^1/_8$	teaspoon thyme
			Salt and pepper
3 to 4	pork tenderloins, about 4 pounds total	1	teaspoon orange juice

MAKES 8 SERVINGS

*I*n a medium saucepan, combine the water, sugar, salt, minced fennel and seeds, thyme, and pepper. Bring the mixture to a boil. Remove from the heat and let cool. Add the orange peel.

Pour the mixture over the tenderloins in a glass dish and soak [marinate], covered, in the refrigerator for about 48 hours.

When ready to serve, heat up the grill. Remove the meat from the marinade and place the loins on the grill. Strain the seasonings from the brine and spread over the coals. Cover the grill and cook the meat for about 5 minutes, turning frequently, until the internal temperature reaches 150° (about 15 to 20 minutes). Let the meat stand for 5 minutes.

While the meat rests, prepare the glaze. In a small sauté pan, melt the butter and sauté the fresh fennel for 3 minutes. Add the honey. Combine the lime with the cornstarch and add it to the butter mixture. Add the remaining ingredients except the orange juice. Cook over medium-high heat, just to incorporate the flavors. Add the orange juice and remove from the heat. Pour over the tenderloins and serve immediately.

JARRETT FARM

[27]

Tuscan Stuffed Veal with Chianti Sauce

The romance of the Toscana hills in Italy's countryside inspired this dish as well as the Chianti Classico made in that region. I toted a bottle of that wine all the way home from Europe not too long ago. This dish is mild and the flavors intense but subtle, just like Tuscany. This dish may also be made with chicken breasts.

Shop in one of those dollar stores and outfit the kitchen with cheap but fun gadgets. You might even find something interesting for a romantic dinner, the least of which may be the conversation you can have over your spree through the store. Buy with abandon. Such pleasure only costs a few dollars!

2	boneless veal cutlets (about 4 ounces each)		1	egg, beaten for egg wash
	White pepper		1/4	cup Italian-seasoned breadcrumbs
2	ounces Taleggio or Fontina cheese, thinly sliced		1	tablespoon extra-virgin olive oil
1	red bell pepper, roasted and cut julienne		3/4	cup Chianti or other full-bodied dry red wine
6	sage leaves, freshly chopped		1 1/2	tablespoons cornstarch mixed with 1 tablespoon cold water
1/4	cup chopped black olives			
1	clove garlic, minced			

MAKES 2 SERVINGS

Lightly pound the veal to 1/4-inch thick. Season lightly with the white pepper. Evenly divide the cheese between the 2 pieces of veal. Do the same with the red pep-

pers, sage, olives, and garlic. Roll the veal up jellyroll style, sealing the edges as well as possible.

Lightly brush with the egg wash and coat with the bread-crumbs.

In a medium skillet, heat the oil over medium-high heat. Add the stuffed veal and sauté for 5 to 6 minutes, browning on all sides. Remove from the skillet and set aside. Deglaze the pan with the wine. Turn the heat down to a simmer and cook, covered, for about 2 minutes, to reduce slightly. Return the veal to the pan and cook the veal in the wine covered for about 5 minutes more or until the veal is cooked medium or well, according to desired doneness. Remove from the pan and add the cornstarch mixture, if desired, to thicken the sauce. Serve immediately.

GAIL'S KITCHEN

Sage and Garlic Rubbed Steak with Gorgonzola Butter

ﾟﾟﾟ

Serve this creative and flavorful steak with a few small red potatoes and some sugar snap peas. Rabbit Hill Inn is one of America's most romantic places.

Garlic rub			Steaks	
1/4	cup cumin		2	8-ounce ribeye steak filets
1/4	cup garlic powder			
1	teaspoon freshly cracked black pepper		*Gorgonzola butter*	
1	teaspoon salt		1/2	cup (1 stick) unsalted butter
1/2	tablespoon onion powder		1/4	cup minced shallots
1	tablespoon ground dried sage		1/2	tablespoon minced garlic
1	tablespoon minced dried basil		3	ounces Gorgonzola cheese
1/2	tablespoon cumin seed, optional		1/8	tablespoon salt
1/2	tablespoon powdered mustard		1/8	teaspoon freshly ground black pepper

MAKES 2 SERVINGS

In a resealable container, combine all the ingredients for the garlic rub. Mix well. Pour enough of the spice mixture to coat the steaks on a flat plate or platter. Dredge the filets in the seasoning, completely covering both sides. (Discard any excess seasoning but cover and store any unused seasoning for future use.) Set aside and prepare the Gorgonzola butter.

In a food processor, purée the butter until soft. Add the shallots, garlic, cheese, salt, and pepper. Continue to mix until well blended. Return to the refrigerator just to chill. Grill the steaks about 6 minutes on each side or to desired doneness. Scoop out 2 tablespoons of the Gorgonzola butter and place on the top of each steak. Reserve leftover seasoned butter for another recipe.

RABBIT HILL INN

[30]

Pistachio-Crusted Scallops with Papaya Sauce

⌘

The delicate, subtle flavor of the nuts with the soothing taste of the fruit makes for a dish that goes well with a side of asparagus spears and julienned carrots. Avoid pistachio shells that are not partially opened, as the nut is immature.

Scallops		Sauce	
	12 to 16 sea scallops (about 2 pounds)	2	cups dry white wine
	Salt and freshly cracked pepper	2	teaspoons white vinegar
1	cup pistachios, shelled and coarsely chopped	2	shallots, finely chopped
		1	cup papaya (about 2 small papayas), cut into a small dice
		2	cups light or heavy cream
		1/2	cup (1 stick) unsalted butter, cut into 1-inch cubes

MAKES 4 SERVINGS

Preheat the oven to 400°. Place a cast-iron skillet over a high flame. Season the scallops with salt and pepper. When the skillet is hot, add the scallops and sear on both sides until well-browned. Remove the scallops from the pan and place them in an oven-proof dish. Top with the chopped pistachios. Cook covered 5 to 6 minutes or until firm. (Do not overcook.)

Meanwhile, begin the sauce preparation. Combine the white wine, vinegar, shallots, and papaya in a small saucepan. Cook the sauce over medium-high heat until the mixture takes on a syrupy consistency. Add the cream and continue cooking until the mixture is reduced by half. Remove the pan from the heat and whisk in the butter cubes until melted and incorporated. To serve, ladle sauce in the center of each plate. Arrange 3 to 4 scallops in the center of each plate. Reserve any leftover sauce for another recipe.

MERCERSBURG INN

Sesame-Crusted Halibut
with Lemon-Sage Butter

≈≈

Chef Sam Chapman finishes the halibut by baking it on a piece of alder wood (about 8 inches in diameter) or other flavored woods such as berry, hickory, maple, cedar, and birch. American Indians used native trees instead of pottery to cook fish. Cooking fish on wood offers a hint of charred wood, similar to a barbecue or charred wood flavor. Many home improvement stores carry wood for cooking. Although it does not have as much flavor, this dish is still good cooked in a baking pan. The recipe makes extra sage butter for future use.

Butter		Halibut	
1/2	cup (1 stick) butter, softened	1	cup sesame seeds
1/2	tablespoon chopped fresh sage leaves	1/4	cup all-purpose flour
	Juice and grated peel of 1/4 lemon		Salt and white pepper
		2	6-ounce halibut filéts
1/2	tablespoon minced garlic	1	tablespoon olive oil for sautéing
			Sage sprigs and lemon wedges for garnish

MAKES 2 SERVINGS

*P*reheat the oven to 400°. Make the sage butter. Place all of the ingredients in a small bowl of electric mixer and whip until fluffy and all ingredients are incorporated. Shape into a 12-inch log and wrap in waxed paper. Refrigerate until solidified.

Mix together the sesame seeds and flour. Season with salt and pepper. Dredge the filéts in the mixture. Heat the olive oil and sauté the halibut in a medium ovenproof nonstick sauté pan on high heat, browning both sides, about 2 minutes per side. Place the halibut on the wood and place in the oven to bake 15 minutes or until the flesh feels firm to the touch.

Place the fish in the center of the serving plate. Top the fish with a tablespoon of the sage butter. (Refrigerate the remaining butter for future use.) Garnish with sage and lemon.

THE CAPTAIN WHIDBEY INN

*H*ere is a simple sensual breakfast beverage: 1 cup vanilla ice cream whipped together with 1 pint orange juice. Don't they call this a creamsicle!

Baked Salmon-and-Mushroom Wellington

≈≈≈

Innkeeper Dennis Hayden is absolutely passionate about cooking and his guests reap the benefits. This is a cinch to prepare ahead of time before your guests arrive.

Salmon

3	cups water
1	cup white vinegar
2	8-ounce salmon filets (with skin on)

Filling

2	cups fresh spinach
1/4	teaspoon extra virgin olive oil
1	small onion, finely chopped
6	medium button mushrooms, cleaned and thinly sliced

Assembly

2	3x6-inch rectangles cut from a sheet of frozen puff pastry dough, thawed
1	egg yolk
	Hollandaise sauce
	Fresh dill

MAKES 2 SERVINGS

*I*n a large, deep skillet set over high heat, combine the water and vinegar. Bring to a boil. Add the salmon and poach for 5 to 10 minutes, depending on the thickness of the filets. Remove the salmon, pat dry, and set aside.

Preheat the oven to 400°. Meanwhile, prepare the filling. Wash and drain the spinach, squeezing well to drain all the moisture. Steam the leaves in a small amount of water until wilted. Discard the excess water and coarsely chop the cooked spinach leaves. In a small skillet over medium-high heat, heat the olive oil. When the oil is hot, add the chopped onions and mushroom slices. Sauté the mixture for a few minutes or until the onions are translucent. Transfer the onions and mushrooms to a food processor. Add the spinach and pulse until the filling mixture is finely chopped and thoroughly mixed.

To assemble the dish, cut the thawed puff pastry into 3x6-inch rectangles. Spread the filling mixture evenly on each pastry. Add a salmon filet and gently wrap the pastry around the salmon. Pinch the ends of the dough together, forming a seam. Arrange the salmon—seam side down—on a baking sheet. Prepare an egg wash by whipping the egg yolk with a few drops of cold water. Brush the salmon bundles with the mixture for a golden brown result. Bake for 20 to 25 minutes or until golden brown. Serve with Hollandaise sauce and fresh dill.

BLUE HARBOR HOUSE

Baked French Chicken Casserole

❦

Such a standby but elegant dish as this one almost guarantees a successful dinner. Nice served with sautéed zucchini and fried rice.

1	tablespoon butter	1	medium ripe Roma tomato, seeded and cut into $1/2$-inch dice
1	clove garlic, minced		
$1/4$	cup all-purpose flour	2	tablespoons chopped flat-leaf parsley
2	whole boneless, skinless chicken breasts, pounded to $1/4$-inch thick		
		$1/4$	cup light cream
	Salt and pepper	$1/2$	cup shredded Mozzarella cheese
$1/2$	cup sliced mushrooms		

MAKES 2 SERVINGS

*P*reheat the oven to 350°. In a sauté pan, melt the butter over medium-high heat. Add the garlic and sauté for about 3 minutes. Meanwhile, sprinkle the flour on a plate. Dredge the chicken breasts, coating both sides. Season with salt and pepper. Add the chicken to the pan and cook until browned on both sides.

    Coat a baking dish with cooking oil spray. Transfer the browned chicken breasts to the dish. Sprinkle the mushrooms, tomatoes, and parsley over the chicken breasts. Pour the cream over the chicken, distributing evenly. Bake in the oven for 30 minutes or until golden brown. Remove from the oven and sprinkle with Mozzarella cheese. Bake for an additional 10 minutes or until the cheese has melted.

VICTORIAN OAKS

*V*isit a bakery and inhale the sweet-scented pleasures of baking confections. 'Twill brighten any day.

Chicken Chèvre Pâtisserie

❧◦❧

Goat cheese may be purchased plain or crusted with herbs, or you can add your own herbal assortment. At Squire Tarbox they produce their own cheese from the milk of very loved Nubian goats, who are a part of the welcoming committee at the inn. Guests can watch innkeeper Karen Mitman milk the goats twice a day. I highly recommend calling for her mail-order cheese brochure.

LEFT: THE SQUIRE TARBOX INN, WISCASSET, MAINE

Chicken Chèvre Pâtisserie (continued)

4	small boneless, skinless chicken breasts
4	ounces herbed Chèvre (goat cheese)
4	sheets frozen puff pastry, thawed
	Salt and freshly cracked pepper
1	egg yolk, beaten

MAKES 4 SERVINGS

P̲reheat the oven to 425°. Wash and drain chicken breasts. Pat dry. Roll out a puff pastry sheet to about ¹/₄ inch and arrange on a flat surface. Place 1 chicken breast on the dough, about 2 inches from the top. Season with salt and pepper. You may cut out

little hearts with a tiny cookie cutter, using the excess dough. Spread 1 tablespoon or so of the Chèvre on the chicken breast. Roll the pastry around the chicken, folding in the sides as you go. Pinch the seams together, sealing with a few drops of warm water. (Add a heart, if desired, at this point, sealing with water, placing the heart in the center, top of the pastry.) Using a fork, puncture the top of the puff pastry to allow air to circulate during cooking. Brush with the beaten egg yolk. Continue with the remaining chicken breasts.

Place the pastry-wrapped chicken breasts on a greased cookie sheet. Bake for 25 minutes or until golden brown. Let stand for 10 minutes before serving.

THE SQUIRE TARBOX INN

RIGHT: THE FORMER SPRING HOUSE AT INN AT VAUCLUSE SPRING IS NOW A GUEST HOUSE.

Rosemary and Apple Cider-Glazed "Love" Hens

~o~

Innkeeper/chef Neil Myers even makes the cooking process a romantic one with her recipes. In this one she calls for basting game hens—not with a brush but with branches of rosemary. (Neil says everyone at the inn calls these "love" hens.) The Inn at Vaucluse Spring is located in fruit-orchard country, and nearby, fresh apple cider is pressed.

Glaze

1/2	gallon pressed cider, boiled down to 1/2 quart
1/4	cup Dijon-style mustard
1/4	cup pure honey or lavender honey
1/4	cup light soy sauce
2	tablespoons apple cider vinegar
1	6-inch branch fresh rosemary, for basting

Hens

3	game hens
1/2	tart apple, unpeeled, cored, and divided into 6 equal slices
2	thin green onions, trimmed, cut in half lengthwise
3	tablespoons raisins
3	2-inch cinnamon sticks
3	2-inch sprigs fresh rosemary, plus 6 1-inch sprigs for garnish
	Paprika
	Salt and freshly cracked pepper
1	medium red apple, cut into thin slices, for garnish

MAKES 6 SERVINGS

In a large nonstick skillet, combine the reduced cider, mustard, honey, soy sauce, cider vinegar, and rosemary. Stir over medium heat until reduced to a glaze consistency, about 30 minutes.

Preheat the oven to 325°. Line a baking sheet with foil and coat with cooking oil spray. Stuff each hen with an apple slice, half an onion, 1 tablespoon of the raisins, 1/2 cinnamon stick, and a 2-inch sprig of rosemary. Sprinkle with paprika, salt, and pepper. Place the hens breast-side down on the pan and bake in the oven for 30 minutes. Turn the hens over and return to the oven in reversed position for even cooking. Bake another 15 minutes and then baste the hens with the cider glaze, using the large rosemary branch. (Reserve remaining glaze for serving.) Cook the hens for another 45 minutes. Using the rosemary, continue basting every 10 to 15 minutes with the pan drippings.

When the hens are cooked to a golden brown (about 1 1/2 hours) remove them from the oven and cut in half. Heat the remaining glaze. (Remove the cinnamon stick and rosemary sprig from the hen stuffing.) Pool a little glaze onto each serving plate and place half a hen, bone-side down, on the glaze. Ladle on a little more glaze and garnish with the apple slices and a sprig of rosemary.

THE INN AT VAUCLUSE SPRING

Elderberry and Ginger Duckling

∽o∾

The purple-black fruits of the elderberry tree yield a velvety sauce for this elegant duck. Imagine a dining room in a Victorian parlor with quiet conversation and flickering candles. That's what it is like here at the inn during dinner.

THE SAUSAGE-AND-MUSHROOM-STUFFED PILLOWS (RECIPE ON PAGE 18) ARE PICTURED TO THE LEFT OF THE PLATE.

4	duckling halves (12 ounces each)
3	tablespoons sugar
1/3	cup cider vinegar
1	cup elderberry preserves or substitute with blueberry
3	tablespoons brandy
1	tablespoon butter
1	teaspoon freshly grated ginger (or 1/2 teaspoon ground ginger)

MAKES 4 SERVINGS

*P*reheat the oven to 350°. Arrange the duckling halves in a roasting pan. Bake for 25 to 30 minutes or until the duckling is tender and the skin crispy.

While the duck bakes, prepare the sauce. In a heavy saucepan, combine the sugar, vinegar, elderberry preserves, brandy, butter, and ginger. Place over medium heat and bring to a slow boil. Reduce the heat to low and simmer for 5 to 10 minutes, stirring constantly to avoid scorching. Remove from heat and keep warm until serving. Drizzle over duckling.

THE INN AT OLDE NEW BERLIN

*H*ere is a tip from Donecker's Country Inn: ceiling lights detract from romance; cover them with a straw basket and let the light filter over the table like lace.

Dessert

Strawberry Shortbread Shortcakes

∽o∾

Strawberry shortcake was originally made with biscuits for layers, not cakes. This version is made with biscuits of light shortbread, adapted from a recipe that has been in innkeeper Karen Caplanis' family for generations. No matter how you prepare it, strawberry shortcake is always romantic. The flavor of black currants or Chambord, and/or lemon juice, may be added to bring out the sweetness of the berries. Prepare the filling first as it needs some time to set in the refrigerator.

CHAPTER OPENER: TITLES ON A STACK OF BOOKS CROWNED WITH SOMETHING SWEET, DESCRIBE THE ESSENCE OF THE INN AT VAUCLUSE SPRING.

Filling

2	quarts fresh strawberries, cleaned and hulled (reserve 6 berries for garnish)
1/4	cup lightly packed brown sugar
1/4	cup sugar
	Strawberry preserves
	Crème de Cassis or Chambord

Shortbread shortcakes

1	cup all-purpose flour
1 1/2	rounded teaspoons baking powder
1/4	teaspoon salt
1 1/2	tablespoons sugar
3 1/2	tablespoons chilled butter
1	small egg, slightly beaten
1/4	cup milk

Assembly

2	cups or so whipped cream for garnish
6	mint leaves for garnish

MAKES 6 SHORTCAKES

In a blender, purée 1 cup of strawberries with the sugars, and if berries are not sweet enough, add the preserves and/or the liqueur to desired sweetness. Slice the remaining berries and add to the purée. Refrigerate for 2 hours before serving.

When ready to serve, preheat the oven to 400°. Coat a cookie sheet with nonstick cooking oil spray. In a large bowl, sift together the flour, baking powder, salt, and sugar. Cut the butter in with a pastry blender. Make a well in the center. Beat together the egg and milk and pour into the well, mixing just until blended. Drop by the rounded tablespoonful, making 3-inch circles, using up all of the batter to form 6 biscuits. Bake for 9 to 12 minutes or until golden brown. Let cakes cool to room temperature on a wire rack.

To serve, split the shortcakes in half. Place the bottom halves on a serving plate and spoon the strawberry mixture on them. Add the top of the biscuits to form a sandwich. Pour remaining berries overtop. Add a dollop of whipped cream, a whole strawberry, and a mint leaf.

THE INN AT VAUCLUSE SPRING

Iced Mocha Cappuccino Cheesecake

⚜

Something between a *café au lait* and coffee ice cream, this luscious cheesecake provides just the right romantic flavor. If you visit the inn, this cake might be served to you in what was once the front parlor. With the decor and fine service, you'll feel as if you are back in the nineteenth century.

Whenever you are near fresh herbs, rub them with your thumb and index finger to delight in their fresh scents.

LEFT: THE CHEESECAKE AND THE FOYER OF THE INN AT OLDE NEW BERLIN

Iced Mocha Cappuccino Cheesecake (continued)

Crust

1 1/2	cups finely chopped pecans
3	tablespoons butter, melted
1	cup plus 2 tablespoons sugar

Cake

4	(8-ounce) packages cream cheese, softened
3	tablespoons all-purpose flour
4	eggs
1	cup sour cream
1/4	teaspoon ground cinnamon

1	tablespoon instant coffee granules
1/4	cup orange juice

Topping

1	cup mini chocolate chips
1/3	cup heavy cream
2	tablespoons espresso, or very strong coffee

MAKES 8 TO 10 SERVINGS

*P*reheat the oven to 350°. In a large bowl, combine the nuts, the butter, and 2 table-spoons of the sugar. Stir well until all the crust ingredients are incorporated. Pour into a 9-inch springform pan and press firmly onto the bottom and up the sides of the pan by about 2 inches, or so. Set aside.

In a food processor, combine the cream cheese and the remaining cup of sugar. Process until the mixture is light and completely combined. Stir in the flour, and then the eggs— one at a time. When smooth, blend in the sour cream and cinnamon.

In a small dish, combine the instant coffee and orange juice. Stir until the granules dissolve. Add to the cream cheese mixture, stirring well to blend. Pour the cheesecake batter into the prepared pan. Bake at 350° for about 1 hour or until a tester comes clean. Cool completely before removing from the pan.

When the cake is cooled, prepare the topping. In a medium saucepan, heat the choco-late chips, heavy cream, and espresso. Stir until the chocolate has melted and the ingredients are completely combined. Let cool to room temperature and spread over the top of the cake. Refrigerate the cake until ready to serve.

THE INN AT OLDE NEW BERLIN

Chocolate Hazelnut Torte

❦

Serve this delicious layered dessert for an elegant dinner party. Just looking at it arouses the senses with its buttercream filling and chocolate icing or ganache.

Torte

1/2	cup pastry flour
1 1/2	teaspoons baking powder
8	ounces bittersweet chocolate
1	cup (2 sticks) unsalted butter, softened
1	cup sugar
8	eggs, separated
1	cup finely chopped hazelnuts, plus 2 whole nuts for garnish

Filling

1/2	cup (1 stick) butter, softened
2	tablespoons powdered sugar
1/2	cup raspberry preserves

Ganache

10	ounces bittersweet chocolate
1	cup heavy cream

MAKES 16 SERVINGS

In a small bowl, mix together the flour and the baking powder. Melt the chocolate in a double boiler. In a large bowl, cream together the butter and sugar. Then add the egg yolks one at a time, followed by the nuts. Add the chocolate to the butter mixture, then add the flour mixture. Set aside.

Preheat the oven to 325°. In a separate bowl, whip the egg whites until stiff peaks form. Fold the egg whites into the batter until fully mixed.

Prepare 2 9-inch round cake pans with cooking oil spray. Cover with parchment paper. Spray paper and sprinkle with flour. Evenly divide the cake mixture between pans. Bake 30 minutes or until tester comes clean. Cool at room temperature.

While the layers bake, prepare the cream filling. In small bowl of electric mixer, cream together the butter and powdered sugar. Add the preserves and mix until fully incorporated. Spread the cream filling on top of 1 of the layers. Place the other layer on top of the first layer. Set aside and prepare the icing.

Melt the chocolate with the cream over medium heat, stirring constantly until the mixture thickens. Immediately pour the ganache over the torte, making sure to cover the entire torte—top and sides. Let set to cool and harden. Add whole hazelnuts for garnish.

THE WINCHESTER COUNTRY INN

Sweet Chèvre Pound Cake

✧◦✧

The Chèvre or goat cheese in this recipe does what sour cream does in a pound cake, making a moister texture and a slightly more intense taste. Made with goat's milk, this cheese is healthier than sour cream, often used in pound cake. This cake freezes well. The Squire Tarbox is one of America's most traditional country inns. It should not be missed.

1 ⅓	cups soft goat cheese (or cream cheese)
2	cups (4 sticks) butter, softened
2 ⅔	cups sugar
⅛	teaspoon salt
1	tablespoon lemon extract
8	eggs
4	cups all-purpose flour
	Strawberries for garnish

MAKES 2 CAKES

*P*reheat the oven to 325°. Butter and flour 2 (10-inch) tube pans. In a large mixer bowl, blend the goat cheese and the butter. Then, with the mixer on high speed, add the sugar, salt, and lemon extract, beating until the mixture is smooth and light. Add the eggs—one at a time, continuing to beat until fluffy. Reduce the speed to low and

add the flour, mixing until just combined. Divide the batter evenly between the pans. Bake for 1 hour and 15 minutes or until a tester comes clean. Remove the cakes from the oven and allow to cool for 5 minutes before inverting onto wire racks. Serve with fresh strawberries or a pool of puréed raspberries.

INNKEEPER KAREN MITMAN AND ABBI

THE SQUIRE TARBOX INN

Chocolate Raisin Pie

∽◦∾

When I used to eat candy-store candy bars, Chunky bars were my favorite. I have
always enjoyed the combination of chocolate and raisins. So this pie is buttery and
chocolate. It reminds me of simple times, such as the day I spent lingering at the view
from my room at the Lodge on Lake Lure.

2	eggs	1	cup chocolate chips
1/2	cup all-purpose flour	1	cup coarsely chopped walnuts
1/2	cup sugar	1/2	cup raisins
1/2	cup firmly packed brown sugar	1	9-inch pie shell
			Whipped cream for garnish
1	cup (2 sticks) butter, melted and cooled		

MAKES 1 (9-INCH) PIE

*Preheat the oven to 325°. In a large bowl beat the
eggs until foamy. Add flour, sugar, and brown sugar.
Beat until well blended. Blend in the melted butter.
Stir in the chocolate chips, walnuts, and raisins.
Pour into the pie shell. Bake for 1 hour or until the
top is golden brown. Serve with a dollop of whipped
cream if desired.*

GAIL'S KITCHEN

SNAPSHOT OF A PLEASANT AND ROMANTIC
TIME AT CASA SEDONA IN SEDONA, ARIZONA

MEMORIES OF A STAY AT GRAHAM'S B&B IN SEDONA, ARIZONA

*In the childhood memories of every good cook, there's a large kitchen,
a warm stove, a simmering pot, and a mom.*
— *Barbara Costikyan*

Coconut Coffee Ice Cream Pie with Oreo Crust and Amaretto-Chocolate Sauce

❦

I love coffee ice cream, and I love chocolate, and who doesn't love Oreo cookies. Here it is the best of romance from a romantic spot, a hilltop retreat complete with rockers on the porch. The recipe needs several hours for freezing time.

Beg the folks at Run of the River B&B to send you their uplifting newsletter even if you have never visited this enchanting place. One way Monty and Karen reach out to their guests is by giving them ideas for simple pleasures: throw a snowball, make a toast by firelight, drink in the aroma of fresh-ground coffee, hug a sleigh horse. These are things you find in the newsletter of Run of the River to do there, or at home—if you miss your plane to the Leavenworth, Washington, area.

Sauce			Pie	
1 1/2	cups whipping cream		1 1/2	cups crumbled Oreo cookies
2/3	cup brown sugar		1/4	cup (1/2 stick) butter, melted
3	ounces semisweet chocolate		1/2	cup slivered almonds, toasted
4	ounces unsweetened chocolate		1 1/2	cups unsweetened coconut, toasted
1/4	cup (1/2 stick) butter, softened		1 1/2	pints coffee ice cream
1	tablespoon Amaretto or Frangelico		1/4	cup sweetened condensed milk
			2	cups heavy cream, chilled
			1/2	teaspoon vanilla extract
			1/2	teaspoon Amaretto

MAKES 8 SERVINGS

Combine the cream and brown sugar over a double boiler. Whisk occasionally, dissolving the brown sugar. Add the chocolates and whisk the mixture until the chocolate is melted. Whisk in the butter and liqueur until the sauce is smooth. Set aside. (Reheat when serving the pie.)

Finely chop the cookies in a food processor. Add the melted butter and mix well. Pat the mixture into the bottom of an 8-inch springform pan and freeze until firm.

When the crust is frozen (15 to 30 minutes), turn the oven broiler on. Place the almonds on a baking sheet and toast lightly. On another sheet, toast the coconut, watching carefully to prevent burning. Stir occasionally to brown evenly. Set both aside to cool. Allow the ice cream to soften to a spreading consistency and spread evenly on the crust. Freeze until firm, about 30 minutes. In a medium mixing bowl combine the coconut and milk. Set aside.

In a large bowl of electric mixer, beat the cream until soft peaks form. Add the vanilla and Amaretto and beat until stiff. Gradually fold in the coconut mixture and spread over the coffee ice cream. Sprinkle the toasted almonds over the whipped mixture. Cover the pie and freeze at least 4 hours or overnight.

To serve, wrap a dampened kitchen towel around the side of the pan. Remove the side. Place a pool of warmed sauce on a serving plate. Cut the pie into wedges and serve.

JARRETT FARM

[59]

Baked Orange-Almond Custard

⤫

The mixture of the orange and almonds with the delicate texture of the custard is heavenly and rate high on the romance meter.

1/2	cup (1 stick) unsalted butter, softened		Grated peel from 3 oranges, minced
1 1/2	cups sugar	1/2	cup sliced, toasted almonds
6	eggs, separated, at room temperature	1 1/2	cups milk
2/3	cup freshly squeezed orange juice	1 1/2	cups heavy cream
2/3	cup all-purpose flour	1/4	teaspoon salt

MAKES 8 SERVINGS

*P*reheat the oven to 350°. With an electric mixer, cream together the butter and sugar until light and fluffy. Beat in the egg yolks—one at a time. When the yolks are thoroughly incorporated, stir in the orange juice, flour, and almonds. Add the milk and the heavy cream. Mix well until blended.

In a separate bowl, beat the egg whites with the salt until soft peaks form. Gently fold the whites into the butter mixture. Pour the batter into a greased 13x9-inch baking pan. Place the pan in a larger baking dish and fill the baking dish halfway with hot water. Bake for 1 hour. Remove from the oven and cool slightly. Serve warm.

RABBIT HILL INN

GOOD MORNING, FROM THE KING'S COTTAGE IN LANCASTER, PENNSYLVANIA.

Now and then I pick up an antique wedding cake top — the folk art of romance.

Hot Fudge-and-Peanut-Butter Banana Split

∽∾∽

I know, I know, the calories, but take the term "banana split" literally and split this dish between the two of you. It couldn't be more fun. Indulge. There is a recipe here for peanut butter ice cream, but you may want to add two other flavored scoops to this old-fashioned fountain specialty.

"... *There can be no enduring happiness, no real marriage, if a man and woman cannot open themselves generously and without suspicion one to the other over a shared bowl of soup as well as a shared caress.*"
M.F.K. Fisher, House Beautiful, 1948

Peanut butter ice cream		*Topping*	
1 ²/₃	cups milk	1	pint whipping cream
1 ²/₃	cups half-and-half	¹/₄	cup superfine sugar
2	cups peanut butter (smooth or chunky)	2	tablespoons crème de cacao liqueur
1	cup sugar	*Assembly*	
4	teaspoons vanilla extract	1	banana
Sauce		3	scoops ice cream
3	cups heavy cream	1	tablespoon toasted crushed almonds
1 ¹/₂	cups (3 sticks) butter	*Whipped cream*	
1 ¹/₄	cups sugar	1	chocolate-covered cordial of choice
1 ¹/₄	cups lightly packed brown sugar	¹/₄	cup hot fudge sauce
¹/₂	teaspoon sea salt		
2	cups unsweetened cocoa, sifted		

MAKES 2 SERVINGS

*P*repare the ice cream several hours ahead of serving time. In a saucepan, simmer the milk, half-and-half, peanut butter, and sugar, stirring until smooth. Stir in the vanilla and remove from the heat. Let the mixture cool. Pour the mixture into an ice cream machine and proceed to make the ice cream according to your particular machine instructions. Freeze.

When the ice cream has frozen, prepare the fudge sauce. In a small saucepan, combine the cream and butter. Stir over medium heat until the butter is melted and the cream just begins to boil. Add the sugars and stir until sugars are dissolved. Add the salt and cocoa and whisk until smooth. (The sauce yields 6 cups, so store the leftover sauce in the refrigerator for later use.)

Mix together the whipping cream, superfine sugar, and crème de cacao until sugar is dissolved, then whip with an electric mixer or balloon whip until fluffy and creamy.

Cut the banana in half lengthwise (reserve ¹/₂ for another recipe). Cut the split in half and place at either end of a dessert dish, such as the soda fountain-style banana split dishes. Place ice cream scoops in between the bananas. Ladle hot fudge sauce over the ice cream. Top with the flavored whipped cream and sprinkle with nuts. Top with a chocolate cordial and dig in!

THE CAPTAIN WHIDBEY INN

The Romance of Country Inns

The
Morning
After

〜⚮〜

Vanilla Varoom Through a Straw

The innkeepers at Run of the River suggest that feeling romantic is the result of being healthy, so they serve this energy drink as a restorative gift to their guests. Even the name feels like you can get-up-'n'- go.

2	Golden Delicious apples, peeled, cored, and coarsely chopped
2	tablespoons chopped walnuts
2	tablespoons wheat germ
3	tablespoons vanilla low-fat yogurt
1 ½	cups or more apple juice

MAKES 2 SERVINGS

Place the apples, walnuts, wheat germ, and yogurt in a blender. Pour in the apple juice. Blend until smooth, adding more apple juice if a thinner consistency is desired.

RUN OF THE RIVER

Here's a note you can leave at the place setting of your significant other. (Even though it was sent as a birthday greeting, I think it is romantic.) "Thoughts are warm like sunshine, welcome like rainbows, fun like circuses … when they're thoughts of you."

CHAPTER OPENER: THE MORNING AFTER WITH CRÈPE CUPS LORRAINE AT BOXWOOD INN, RECIPE ON PAGE 87

Panama Canal in a Glass

∾∾

The folks at this picturesque inn, surrounded by snow-capped peaks and colorful wildflowers, believe that fruit smoothies are a rite of breakfast and a passage to a great day ahead. I think they have the right idea.

2	oranges, peeled and coarsely chopped	2	tablespoons wheat bran	
4	large strawberries, cleaned and hulled	3	tablespoons Piña Colada-flavored (or substitute with strawberry) low-fat yogurt	
1	ripe banana, cut into sections	1 $1/2$	cups or more orange juice	
2	tablespoons shredded unsweetened coconut			

MAKES 2 SERVINGS

Place the oranges, strawberries, banana, coconut, wheat bran, and yogurt in a blender. Pour in the orange juice. Blend until smooth. Add more juice if desired.

RUN OF THE RIVER

Kissing burns calories.

Plums in Port Wine Sauce

∽∾∾

Primarily produced in the Douro region of Portugal in Vila Nova da Gaia, port is one of the most romantic of all wines because of the attention it receives from winemakers. As one of them in his broken English told me during a visit there, "We care about the port as we care about the child." Innkeeper Marguerite Swanson knows how to bring that nurturing spirit into her B&B mornings.

$^1/_2$	cup sweet port wine
$^1/_2$	cup water
$^1/_4$	cup sugar
1	tablespoon lemon juice
2	3-inch cinnamon sticks
6	whole cloves
5 to 6	large, fresh red-ripe plums
	Whipped cream for garnish

MAKES 4 SERVINGS

In a medium saucepan, heat all of the ingredients except the plums and garnish. Add the plums and bring the mixture to a boil. Reduce the heat and simmer, uncovered, until the plums are tender when pierced with a fork, about 5 minutes.

Remove the plums from the wine mixture and cut them into quarters. (Remove skins if desired) Discard the pits. Meanwhile, return the liquid to a boil, and continue cooking for about 5 minutes. Remove the cinnamon sticks and cloves.

Arrange the plum quarters in individual bowls. Spoon the port wine sauce over the plums and garnish with whipped cream.

DURHAM HOUSE

RIGHT: VIEW FROM THE TOP OF THE TERRACED GARDENS AT LODGE ON LAKE LURE, NORTH CAROLINA

Peaches 'n' Cream-Cheese Bread Pudding with Raspberry Sauce

❦

Homemade bread puddings remind one romantically of childhood days and old-fashioned pleasures. Begin this recipe the night before serving. Our test kitchen was really enamored with this recipe and suggest it as a breakfast dessert but also for a brunch dish. "Yum" as one of our panel chefs put it!

Approach love and cooking with reckless abandon.
—H. Jackson Brown, Life's Little Instruction Book

Pudding

6	cups 1/2-inch plain bread cubes
1	pound low-fat cream cheese, softened
3/4	cup, plus 4 teaspoons sugar
8	eggs
2	cups skim milk
2	teaspoons vanilla extract
1	teaspoon almond extract
2	teaspoons grated lemon peel
1	teaspoon ground cinnamon
1/4	cup sliced almonds
1	pound fresh peaches, cut into 1/4-inch slices (skins intact)

Sauce

10	ounces frozen raspberries
2	tablespoons sugar
1	tablespoon cornstarch

MAKES 12 SERVINGS

*C*oat the bottom and sides of a 9x13-inch baking pan with cooking oil spray. Spread the bread cubes evenly along the bottom of the pan. Set aside.

With an electric mixer, beat the cream cheese with the 3/4 cup of the sugar. When smooth, beat in the eggs. When the mixture is well-blended, add and mix on a low setting the milk, vanilla and almond extracts, and the lemon peel. Continue mixing for about 5 minutes or until smooth and creamy. Pour the mixture evenly over the bread, submerging the cubes. Set aside.

In a small bowl, mix together the remaining 4 teaspoons of sugar and the cinnamon. Sprinkle evenly over the bread, follow with the almonds. Arrange the peaches in rows on the top. Cover with foil and refrigerate overnight.

When ready to serve, preheat the oven to 350°. Uncover the pudding and bake for 1 hour or until set.

Meanwhile, prepare the raspberry sauce. In a small saucepan, heat the berries and sugar over medium heat until hot and juicy. Measure the cornstarch into a small bowl. Spoon a small amount of the hot berry liquid into the bowl and mix thoroughly to create a thin paste. Pour the cornstarch paste back into the hot berries and stir to mix. Continue stirring until thick and bubbly. Spoon the hot sauce over the pudding and serve.

INN AT 410

Blueberry Cottage Pudding

∽∾∿

Imagine having breakfast along the Erie Canal. Dreamy and sumptuous. And that is life at this country inn. Breakfast is delivered to the rooms in baskets at the Canal House. The batter of this pudding forms a cake-like layer on the top. Our test kitchen got carried away on this one, and also tried it adding a crunchy topping of 2 tablespoons of butter mixed with 1/3 cup of flour and 3 tablespoons of sugar. The mixture adds a golden, sugary crunch to the pudding.

6	cups fresh blueberries or frozen (thawed)		$^1/_2$	cup sugar
$^1/_2$	cup honey		2	teaspoons baking powder
2	eggs		$^1/_8$	teaspoon salt
1	tablespoon cornstarch		$^1/_2$	cup milk
1 $^1/_2$	cups all-purpose flour		$^1/_2$	cup (1 stick) unsalted butter, melted

MAKES 6 SERVINGS

Preheat the oven to 375°. Butter a 13x9-inch baking dish. In a large bowl, mix together the blueberries, honey, 1 of the eggs, and the cornstarch. Turn into the prepared dish.

Sift together the flour, sugar, baking powder, and salt. In a separate bowl, combine the milk, butter, and remaining egg. Add to the dry ingredients and stir until just combined. Spoon the batter over the berry mixture in the baking dish, spreading to the edges. Bake for about 45 minutes or until a tester comes clean.

OLIVER LOUD'S CANAL HOUSE INN

LEFT: SCRAMBLED EGGS WITH GROUND SAUSAGE AND CURRY IN A CROISSANT AT THE LODGE ON LAKE LURE.

*A*pple Pie Pizza with Cheddar Cheese Crust

❧

Serve this dish at the table on a wooden pizza peel, and it will put everyone in a cheery mood. It also looks great on a buffet table. Cut into the pie with a pizza wheel. You can also make this in a (10-inch) tart pan.

Offer crusty country breads (never soft breads) when serving a romantic dinner for two. And never slice the bread; bring it whole to the table and break bread together with hands.

Crust

1 1/4	cups all-purpose flour
1	teaspoon salt
1/2	cup (1 stick) butter
1	cup shredded Cheddar cheese
1/4	cup ice water

Topping

1/2	cup powdered non-dairy creamer
1/2	cup lightly packed brown sugar
1/2	cup sugar
1/3	cup sifted all-purpose flour
1/4	teaspoon salt
1	teaspoon ground cinnamon
1/2	teaspoon grated nutmeg
1/4	cup (1/2 stick) butter
6	cups (about 4 medium) apples, peeled cored, and thinly sliced
2	tablespoons lemon juice

MAKES 8 SERVINGS

*P*reheat the oven to 450°. In a large mixing bowl, combine the flour and salt. Cut in the butter until the mixture forms coarse crumbs. Add the cheese and knead by hand until incorporated. Sprinkle ice water over the dough and shape into a ball. Gently pat the dough into a 10-inch circle on a greased pizza pan, turning up the edges to form a crust.

In a small mixing bowl, combine the creamer, sugars, flour, salt, cinnamon, and nutmeg. Sprinkle half the mixture over the prepared crust. With a pastry cutter, cut in the 1/4 cup of butter into remaining mixture, mixing until crumbly. Set aside.

Working from the outer edge to the center, arrange the apple slices along the crust in overlapping, concentric circles. Top the apples with a sprinkling of lemon juice and the butter-sugar crumbs. Bake 30 minutes or until the apples are tender. Serve warm or cold.

WASHINGTON HOUSE INN

Homemade Maple-and-Nut Granola

❧❧❧

If cereal is what you seek for breakfast, granola with its old-fashioned ingredients and made-from-scratch preparation makes the prospect a much more romantic one.

REMEMBERING AN INN MORNING AT THE BUNGAY JAR IN THE
WHITE MOUNTAINS OF NORTHERN NEW HAMPSHIRE

6	cups uncooked old-fashioned oats	1	cup unsweetened shredded coconut
1	cup slivered almonds	2/3	cup canola oil
1	cup coarsely chopped walnuts	2/3	cup honey
1	cup coarsely chopped pecans	1/4	cup pure maple syrup
1	cup sesame seeds	1	cup raisins
1	cup sunflower seeds	1	cup dates
1	cup wheat germ		

MAKES 4 POUNDS

Preheat the oven to 325°. In a large mixing bowl, combine the oats, nuts, seeds, wheat germ, and coconut. Set aside.

In a medium saucepan, cook the oil, honey, and syrup over medium heat until well-blended. Pour the syrup over the dry ingredients and mix well. Spread the mixture on a large baking pan or cookie sheet. Bake for about 30 minutes or until lightly browned, stirring and turning every 10 minutes. Remove the granola from the oven and cool completely. Stir in the raisins and dates. Store in an airtight container at room temperature.

MAPLEWOOD INN

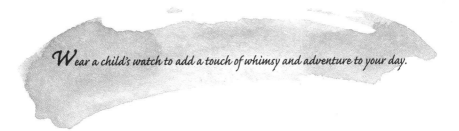

Wear a child's watch to add a touch of whimsy and adventure to your day.

Cinnamon Rolls with "Royal" Icing

∽∾

Someday there's going to be a contest for the best cinnamon rolls and Ravenwood Castle will be among the winners. You can ask a king's ransom in return for one of these. Serve them warm, slathered in a sugar icing that, like this inn, can be called nothing short of "royal" in the true sense of the word.

At Clifton Country Inn, they fold your napkin or get you a fresh one when you need to leave the table momentarily. Nice to do for your guest(s) at home—elegant, romantic.

LEFT: DREAMING OF CINNAMON ROLLS IN RAPUNZEL'S TOWER AT RAVENWOOD CASTLE

Cinnamon Rolls with "Royal" Icing (continued)

Rolls

2	cups very hot water
1/2	cup granulated sugar
2	packages active dry yeast
1/2	teaspoon salt
2	eggs
1/2	cup (1 stick) melted butter
6 to 7	cups all-purpose flour

Filling

1	cup lightly packed brown sugar
2	teaspoons cinnamon
2/3	cup coarsley chopped pecans or walnuts

Icing

1/4	cup (1/2 stick) butter, melted
1/4	cup heavy cream
1	teaspoon vanilla extract
2 to 3	cups sifted powdered sugar or more

MAKES 16 TO 24 BUNS

*I*n a mixing bowl, combine the water, granulated sugar, yeast, salt, eggs, butter, and flour forming a dough that is smooth but not sticky (do not knead). Cover with a tea towel and let rise in a warm place until doubled in size, about 1 hour.

Divide the dough in half and roll each half into a rectangle that is 1/2-inch thick. Spread about 1/4 cup of the butter over each half and sprinkle liberally with the brown sugar, nuts and cinnamon. (Add more of any of these ingredients if desired.) Roll each rectangle up and pinch along the edge to seal. Slice each roll into 8 to 12 slices. Place on greased baking sheets and let rise until doubled again, up to 1 hour.

Bake the rolls in a 375° oven for 18 to 20 minutes until lightly browned.

While the rolls bake, prepare the icing. In a medium mixing bowl, combine the butter, cream, vanilla, and enough powdered sugar to make a spreadable frosting. Remove the rolls from the oven, let cool down slightly Frost and serve.

RAVENWOOD CASTLE

Popovers with Lemon Curd

∞○∞

It may be the images of a quaint English cottage on the edge of a grassy meadow, but popovers suggest romantic scenarios. Why not have them for breakfast! Innkeeper Laura Brasser suggests breaking open the popover and spooning the curd right into the middle of the piping hot Yorkshire pudding. Our testers found these to be light, easy, and refreshing. If you don't have a popover pan, fill muffin tins to the top and bake.

Popovers		*Curd*	
3	eggs	1/2	cup (1 stick) butter
1 1/4	cups nonfat milk		Grated peel and juice of
1 1/4	cups all-purpose flour		2 medium lemons
1/4	teaspoon salt	1	cup sugar
1	tablespoon melted butter	1/8	teaspoon salt
		3	medium eggs

MAKES 6 SERVINGS

*W*hisk the eggs in a large bowl until foamy. Add the milk, flour, salt, and butter. Whisk just until the ingredients are blended. (Some lumps may remain in the batter.)

Butter a popover pan and divide the batter evenly among 6 molds. Place the pan in a cold oven, then immediately set the temperature to 450°. Bake for 20 minutes. Lower the heat to 350° and bake an additional 20 minutes or until the popovers are crisp on the outside.

As the popovers bake, prepare the lemon curd. In a small saucepan, melt the butter slowly over low heat. Place the peelings in a food processor, pulsing 4 to 5 times. Add the sugar and salt, and continue to process until the peel is fine about 2 minutes. Add the lemon juice into the peel mixture. Add the eggs and process 6 to 7 times or until well blended. Transfer the mixture to the saucepan with the melted butter. Stir constantly over high heat just until the pre-boil stage. Maintain high heat, but do not boil. Serve the popovers right out of the oven so that they are warm and crispy.

LORD MAYOR'S INN

Sausage-and-Cheese Breakfast Scones

〜〜〜

These portable, packable breakfast-in-one scones and a thermos of Vanilla Varoom (page 66) or Panama Canal (67) are all you need for an early morning feast somewhere out in nature. Grab walking shoes, a blanket, and a good book, and make it your morning all to yourself. The inn won a first-place breakfast award (with this recipe) from the sausage makers of Jones Dairy Farm.

1	12-ounce package Jones All-Natural Roll Sausage brand, crumbled		2 1/2	teaspoons baking powder
			3/4	cup (1 1/2 sticks) margarine
3 1/4	cups or more all-purpose flour		1 1/2	cups shredded Cheddar cheese
1/2	cup sugar			
1/2	teaspoon salt		3/4	cup buttermilk

MAKES 1 1/2 DOZEN

In a skillet, cook the sausage until lightly browned. Drain on paper towel and set aside. Preheat the oven to 425°. In a large bowl, combine the flour, sugar, salt, and baking powder. With a pastry blender, cut in the margarine until it forms coarse crumbs. Sprinkle in the shredded Cheddar cheese and sausage. Toss lightly. Stir in the buttermilk.

If the dough is too sticky, add a little more flour. With floured hands, knead the dough about 20 times, adding flour as needed. Let the dough rest for about 5 minutes. On a floured surface, press half of the dough into a circle (1/2-inch thick), sealing the edges as you work the dough.

Dip a 2 1/2-inch biscuit cutter in the flour, and press out individual scones from the dough. Repeat with the remaining dough. Place the scones on an ungreased cookie sheet and bake for 10 to 12 minutes. Serve warm with butter.

WASHINGTON HOUSE INN

When guests are coming over, do not have your dog greet them first.

One-Dish Breakfast Risotto

∞

Innkeeper Carol Kirby suggests, "Make this on a morning you'd rather be at the gym. It's a great upper body workout." How true! Risotto takes constant stirring, unlike long-grain rice that cooks on its own. But risotto for breakfast is a splendid idea, and I have a shortcut.

Prepare the ingredients and cook the rice the night before, cooking until just before pouring in the last half cup of milk. Spread the rice out flat on a baking sheet. Cover and refrigerate the rice and the remaining scalded milk. Next morning add the rice to a nonstick saucepan. Add the milk, stirring until incorporated, and then follow the recipe directions for adding the cheese, eggs, and bacon. Serve immediately. You can follow this method with any risotto recipe, and some risotto may be done all at once in a pressure cooker. It only takes a total of 5 minutes and no stirring! This is for a day when you would rather *not* be at the gym.

Take time out to cook over the flames in your fireplace or on hot coals, or at least pop some corn in the hearth.

Risotto

3	tablespoons vegetable oil
2	cups Arborio (short-grain) rice
2	cups boiling water
1	teaspoon salt
4	cups milk

Filling

3	cups (about $3/4$ pound) grated Cheddar cheese
9	hard-boiled eggs, cut into $1/4$-inch slices or thinner
1	pound bacon, cooked crisp and crumbled
	Minced fresh chives for garnish

MAKES 6 TO 8 SERVINGS

*I*n a large saucepan, heat the oil over medium-high heat and add the rice. Stir with a wooden spoon until the rice is coated. Add the boiling water and turn the heat down to a simmer, stirring constantly until most of the water is absorbed. Stir in the salt.

In another large saucepan, scald the milk over medium-low heat. Add $1/2$ cup of the hot milk to the rice and stir constantly until the milk is absorbed. Continue adding the milk, stirring constantly, until all of the milk is absorbed and the rice is al dente, about 20 minutes. Remove the pan from the heat and stir in the cheese. Fold in $2/3$ of the egg slices (reserving some for garnish) and all of the bacon. Season with salt and pepper. Transfer to a serving platter and garnish with egg slices and chives.

SEA CREST BY THE SEA

Baked Crêpe Cups Lorraine

～∞～

Nestled in the bucolic calm of Lancaster County, Boxwood Inn is a special place with some of the friendliest innkeepers you will ever meet. This dish is one of their especially romantic breakfast choices that needs to be prepared at least one hour ahead of serving time. The crêpes are used to line muffin tins and become edible cups for a baked-egg filling.

LEFT: A MOMENT IN TIME INVITES A MEMORY FOR TOMORROW AT BOXWOOD INN

Baked Crêpe Cups Lorraine (continued)

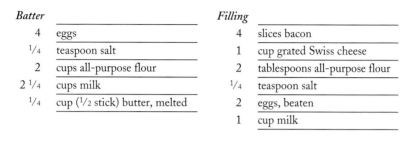

Batter		Filling	
4	eggs	4	slices bacon
1/4	teaspoon salt	1	cup grated Swiss cheese
2	cups all-purpose flour	2	tablespoons all-purpose flour
2 1/4	cups milk	1/4	teaspoon salt
1/4	cup (1/2 stick) butter, melted	2	eggs, beaten
		1	cup milk

MAKES 4 SERVINGS

*I*n a medium bowl, combine the eggs and the salt. Gradually add the flour alternately with the milk, beating until smooth. Beat in the melted butter and refrigerate the batter for 1 hour.

To cook the crêpes, coat a 6-inch frying pan with cooking oil spray. Place the pan over medium high heat. Once the pan is hot, drop 2 to 3 tablespoons of the batter into the pan and tilt the pan until the entire surface is lightly coated with a thin layer of batter. Return the pan to the heat and cook until the crêpe is browned on the bottom. Carefully flip the crêpe with a spatula and brown the remaining side for just a few seconds. Repeat with remaining batter. Gently remove the crêpes and stack them on a plate, separating each crêpe with a sheet of waxed paper.

When the crêpes have cooled, carefully place them in 4 greased muffin tins or custard cups, pressing down to line the molds. Set aside. Preheat the oven to 350°. Cook the bacon until crisp. Crumble the strips into small pieces. Sprinkle into crêpe shells. Top the bacon with a layer of grated Swiss cheese.

Combine the flour, salt, eggs, and milk in a medium bowl. Distribute the mixture evenly over the bacon and cheese in the crêpe shells. Bake for 20 to 30 minutes or until set. Cool for about 5 minutes before removing from the pan. Serve hot.

BOXWOOD INN

A ROMANTIC WAY
TO GREET THE DAY
AT THE OGÉ
HOUSE IN SAN
ANTONIO

Tomato-and-Egg Pesto in Puff Pastry

෴

Simply elegant, this European-inspired dish melts in your mouth, and I like how the inn employs the old-fashioned pesto-making method. Make the pesto in a food processor if you do not have the old tools. Our testers thought this was a great flavor combination to enjoy first thing in the morning.

RIGHT: STONE LOVERS IN A CANOE AT LODGE ON LAKE LURE.

1	package frozen puff pastry (4) shells	*Eggs*		
		8	eggs	
Pesto		¹/₄	cup milk	
1	(2-ounce) bunch fresh basil leaves, plus 2 tablespoons chopped fresh basil	2	tablespoons finely chopped fresh oregano	
2	cloves garlic	2	tablespoons butter	
¹/₈	teaspoon salt	¹/₄	cup shredded Mozzarella cheese	
2	tablespoons pine nuts	¹/₄	cup shredded Monterey Jack or Cheddar cheese	
2	tablespoons Dijon-style mustard	2	tomatoes, seeded and finely diced	
¹/₄	cup grated Parmesan cheese			
¹/₄	cup olive oil			

MAKES 4 SERVINGS

*P*reheat the oven to 425°. Arrange the pastry shells on a foil-coated cookie sheet. Bake for 20 minutes or until golden brown.

Meanwhile, prepare the pesto. Pound the whole basil leaves with the garlic, using

a mortar and pestle (or food processor). Mix in the salt, pine nuts, mustard, and Parmesan cheese. Pound to a thick purée, slowly adding the olive oil until smooth and creamy. Set aside.

In a large mixing bowl, combine the eggs, milk, oregano, and the 2 tablespoons of chopped basil. Beat until well combined. Set aside.

Melt the butter in a large skillet set over medium heat. Pour in the egg mixture. Sprinkle in the shredded cheeses, and then scramble the eggs. When the eggs are just about done, fold in the diced tomatoes. Scoop the eggs into the prepared puff pastry shells.

Drizzle the pesto over the eggs in puff pastry and serve immediately.

SEVEN SISTERS INN

[*91*]

Tomato-Polenta Torte

∽∾∾

Even though this dish hails from Oregon, it brings to mind images of the quiet hill towns of Tuscany. No matter where you serve it, it will conjure up romance, as it does at the Woods House, an inn that is surrounded by the romance of Shakespeare. Ashland, Oregon hosts weeks of Shakespeare festivals every year.

WOODS HOUSE

1/3	cup plus 2 tablespoons olive oil		2	tablespoons fresh oregano, minced
4	large onions, thinly sliced		1	pound fresh spinach, leaves trimmed
	Salt and freshly cracked pepper			Nutmeg
4	cloves garlic, minced		2 1/4	cups instant polenta mix
3	tablespoons pine nuts		1	cup Parmesan cheese
1	28-ounce can Roma tomatoes, drained and chopped			Cayenne pepper
2	tablespoons fresh basil, minced		1/3	cup Italian-seasoned breadcrumbs

MAKES 6 TO 8 SERVINGS

Heat 4 tablespoons of the olive oil in a large skillet. Add the onions and season with salt and pepper. Sauté, stirring occasionally, for about 10 minutes. Stir in half the garlic and cook for 2 more minutes. Toss in the pine nuts. Set aside.

In a medium saucepan, combine 2 tablespoons of the olive oil, the tomatoes, the remaining garlic, basil, and oregano. Season with salt and pepper. Cook over medium heat for about 10 minutes, stirring occasionally, until the mixture is thick.

Meanwhile, place the spinach leaves in a skillet with a little water and heat until just wilted. Drain and squeeze dry. Chop the spinach and place in a bowl. Season with salt, cracked pepper, and nutmeg.

Prepare the polenta according to package directions. Mix in 1 cup of Parmesan cheese, salt, pepper, and cayenne. Transfer 1/3 of the polenta mixture to the bowl with the spinach and mix well. Preheat the oven to 450°. Grease a 9-inch springform pan. Add enough breadcrumbs to coat the bottom and sides of the pan. Spread 1/2 of the remaining polenta along the bottom. Cover with a layer of the onion mixture. Top with remaining polenta. For the next layer, evenly spoon the tomato mixture on top of the polenta, followed by the spinach polenta. Smooth out the polenta and sprinkle with the remaining Parmesan, breadcrumbs, and olive oil.

Bake the torte for 30 minutes or until the top is golden. Let stand at room temperature for at least 5 minutes before releasing the sides of the pan. Serve hot or at room temperature.

THE WOODS HOUSE

Lobster Breakfast Pie

❦

You need to begin this recipe a few hours ahead or the night before.

Pastry

1 1/2	cups all-purpose flour
1/2	cup (1 stick) butter, chilled and cut into 1-inch pieces
1/2	teaspoon salt
1/4	cup ice water

Filling

1	tablespoon butter
1	small onion, chopped
	Salt and freshly cracked pepper
1/8	teaspoon dried red pepper flakes
8	eggs, beaten
2	cups heavy cream
1/4	cup Parmesan cheese
1/2	cup grated Swiss cheese
1	pound shredded cooked lobster meat
1/8	teaspoon paprika
	Fresh parsley for garnish

MAKES 6 SERVINGS

*P*rocess the flour, butter, and salt until the mixture forms coarse cornmeal. Add the ice water and pulse until the dough begins to clump together. Place in a plastic bag and squeeze the bag to press the dough together and into a ball. Continue working the dough into a flat disk. Refrigerate for at least 1 hour or overnight.

Preheat the oven to 450°. Roll the dough onto a lightly floured surface, forming a 1/8-inch-thick circle. Press into an 11-inch pie plate. Bake a few minutes to set. Remove the pie shell from the oven and set aside.

Melt the butter in a nonstick skillet and sauté the onions until tender. Season with salt, pepper, and red pepper flakes. In a large mixing bowl, blend eggs and cream. When combined, stir in the onions, cheeses, and lobster meat. Pour the filling mixture into the prepared pie shell and sprinkle with paprika. Bake for about 10 minutes, then reduce heat to 325° and bake 15 to 20 minutes or until the center is set. Garnish with fresh parsley and serve.

DIAMOND DISTRICT INN

*P*uff *Pear Pancake*

∽◦∾

Because romance is also felt with the eyes, Woods House prepares this eye-opener that may be served with a maple or a fruit syrup of choice. The licorice flavor of the anise seed perfumes the sweet pears gently but boldly.

2	tablespoons butter		5	eggs, separated
1	teaspoon anise seed		1/2	cup sugar
3	large, ripe Bartlett or Anjou pears, peeled, cored, and sliced in half lengthwise		1/2	teaspoon vanilla extract
			1/4	cup all-purpose flour

MAKES 6 SERVINGS

In a 10-inch oven-proof skillet, melt the butter over medium heat. Add the anise seeds and the pears. Cook the pears for about 10 minutes or until browned on both sides. When browned, remove the pan from the heat and turn the pears cut-side-down, and arrange them symmetrically around the pan.

In a large mixing bowl, whip the egg whites until foamy. Gradually add the sugar, continuing to beat until stiff peaks form. Beat the yolks in a separate bowl until doubled in volume. Stir the vanilla and flour into the yolks and beat until well-mixed. Next, stir about 1/4 of the egg whites into the yolks, then fold the entire yolk mixture into the remaining whites.

Preheat the oven to 300°. Pour the egg mixture over the warm pears in the frying pan, pushing the batter down between the fruit pieces. Cook over medium heat until the bottom of the pancake is dark brown, about 10 minutes. Transfer the pan to the oven and bake for about 15 minutes or until the top is golden-brown and the center is set. Gently loosen the pancake from the sides of the pan with a spatula. Place a flat plate over the pan and quickly invert the pancake. Cut into 6 wedges and serve.

THE WOODS HOUSE

Gingerbread-Raisin Pancakes with Lemon Sauce

∽◦∾

Served any time of year, these pancakes force a youthful smile when they are placed in front of your guest. The lemon sauce complements the aroma and flavor of the comforting gingerbread and I like the idea of adding raisins to pancakes.

Lemon Sauce			
3/4	cup (1 1/2 sticks) butter	1 1/2	teaspoons salt
1	cup sugar	1	teaspoon baking soda
1	cup water	2	teaspoons ground cinnamon
3	teaspoons cornstarch	3/4	teaspoon ground ginger
	Grated peel and juice of 3 lemons	1/4	cup dark molasses
		2	cups milk
Pancakes		2	eggs
2 1/2	cups all-purpose flour	6	tablespoons butter, melted
2	teaspoons baking powder	1/2	cup raisins

MAKES 4 SERVINGS

In a large skillet, melt the butter over medium heat. Add the sugar, water, cornstarch, lemon peel, and lemon juice. Stir until the consistency of syrup. Set aside.

In a large mixing bowl, combine all the pancake ingredients except the raisins. Beat until well blended. Stir in the raisins. Drop 2 tablespoons of batter per pancake on a hot griddle or skillet. Cook the pancakes until bubbles form on the surface. Turn, and continue cooking until the cakes are golden brown. Serve with the lemon sauce.

THE BLUE WHALE INN

Carrot Pecan Pancakes

✎✎✎

Nutritious as well as inspirational, these pancakes need to be prepared at least an hour ahead of time. Serve warm with a syrup or fruit purée. This inn is tucked into a time-less street in the heart of uplifting Nashville.

1 1/2	cups all-purpose flour		2	eggs
1	teaspoon baking powder		1	cup buttermilk
1/2	teaspoon salt		2	tablespoons vegetable oil
1/2	teaspoon baking soda		1/2	cup grated carrots
2	tablespoons sugar		1/2	cup coarsely chopped
1/2	teaspoon ground cinnamon			pecans, extra for garnish

MAKES 12 TO 15 PANCAKES

In a large mixing bowl, sift together the flour, baking powder, salt, baking soda, sugar, and cinnamon.

Beat the eggs in a smaller bowl, then stir in the buttermilk. Add the egg mixture to the dry ingredients, mixing well. Add the oil and continue to mix until smooth. Set the batter aside and let stand at room temperature for at least 1 hour.

When the time has elapsed, fold in the grated carrots and the nuts. Heat a lightly oiled griddle over medium-high heat. Spoon 2 tablespoons of the batter into the pan and cook until bubbles appear on the surface. Flip and cook on the reverse side until cakes are golden-brown and all of the batter is used.

THE HILLSBORO HOUSE

Nutty Cheese-and-Apricot-Stuffed French Toast with Gingered-Peach Syrup

◊

Crunchy and buttery-tasting, this dish is largely prepared a day ahead. You can wake up in the morning, and your entrée is practically ready for you. The toast is coated with cornflakes, but I have also enjoyed this dipped in coarsely chopped pecans.

When setting a table for two, create the place setting on an elegant tray. Afterwards, just pick up the tray and bring it to the kitchen; then you can get on with the other important charms of the evening. A nice idea for dinner parties, too.

8	(2-inch thick) slices French bread		1	cup cornflake crumbs or coarsely ground pecans
			2	tablespoons butter

Filling

3/4	cup (3 ounces) shredded Mozzarella cheese
1/2	8-ounce package cream cheese, softened
1	tablespoon Ricotta cheese
3	tablespoons apricot jam or preserves

Toast

2	eggs, lightly beaten
1/2	cup milk

Topping

1	12-ounce bottle apricot or peach syrup
1/4	cup (1/2 stick) butter
2	tablespoons sugar
2	teaspoons ground ginger
16	1/4-inch thin peach slices
	Powdered sugar for garnish

MAKES 8 SERVINGS

*P*reheat the oven to 400°. Starting from one side, split each bread slice, leaving the opposite side attached. Using a fork, hollow out a shallow pocket on the inside of each slice. Set aside.

Combine the cheeses in a mixing bowl. Stir in the jam. Spoon about 2 tablespoons of the filling mixture into each bread slice. Arrange the bread in a 13x9-inch baking dish. Cover and refrigerate 8 hours.

In a large bowl, combine the eggs and milk. Dip each stuffed bread slice into the batter, turning to coat evenly. Spread the cornflake crumbs on a plate and cover the egg-coated bread slices with the flakes on both sides.

Melt 2 tablespoons of butter in a large skillet over medium heat. Cook the French toast for about 2 minutes on each side or until golden brown. Transfer the browned slices to a (clean) lightly greased 13x9-inch baking dish. Bake 15 minutes or until golden brown. Prepare the topping while the French toast bakes. In a small saucepan, heat the apricot syrup. Remove from heat but keep warm. Combine the butter, sugar, and ginger in a large skillet over medium heat. Add the peaches and sauté for about 3 minutes, stirring gently.

Arrange French toast on individual serving plates. Top each serving with sautéed peach slices and dust with powdered sugar. Serve with the warm apricot syrup.

SEVEN SISTERS INN

Directory

Bear Creek Lodge
1184 Bear Creek Trail
Victor, MT 59875
(406) 642-3750

Rooms: 8

    The massive log construction of this lodge makes the inn oh, so perfectly rustic and suited to its location in an area ideal for all manner of outdoor wilderness activities and cozy indoor interlude. This has become one of my all-time favorite inns.

Beckmann Inn
222 East Guenther Street
San Antonio, TX 78204
(210) 229-1449

Rooms: 5

    The inn is one of many splendid buildings in a small neighborhood of breathtaking Texas homes and is within walking distance of the Riverwalk and a few intriguing café-style restaurants.

Blue Harbor House
67 Elm Street
Camden, ME 04843
(207) 236-3196

Rooms: 10

    The inn's brochure says Camden is where the mountains meet the sea. What better place to be?

Blue Whale Inn
6736 Moonstone Beach Drive
Cambria, CA 93428
(805) 927-4647

Rooms: 6

    The inn is situated on bluffs overlooking the Pacific and is close to the famed castle William Randolph Hearst built so that he could enjoy this view as well.

Boxwood Inn
P.O. Box 203
Akron, PA 17501
(717) 859-3466

Rooms: 5

    The Carriage House is my favorite room and overlooks the spacious front lawn of this inn, tucked into the Amish countryside. Splendid. Warm. Refreshing and very friendly.

Captain Whidbey Inn
2072 West Captain Whidbey Inn Road
Coupeville, WA 98239
(206) 678-4097

Rooms: 32

    This 1907 log inn overlooks Penn Cove from the wooded shoreline of Whidbey Island.

Clifton Country Inn
Route 13, Box 26
Charlottesville, VA 22901
804-971-1800

Rooms: 14

    They toast Thomas Jefferson here frequently, as the inn once was the home of Jefferson's daughter, Martha. Dinner is superb, and don't miss afternoon tea.

Diamond District B & B
142 Ocean Street
Lynn, MA 01902
(617) 599-4470

Rooms: 8

    Have a full breakfast on antique English china with a view of the ocean from this Georgian-style clapboard mansion, and you forget the issues of the day and focus on what really matters.

Doneckers Country Inn
318 North State Street
Ephrata, PA 17522
(717) 733-8696

Rooms: 36

A rather large country inn in different buildings, including some that host the inn's own shops. Fun to browse and buy.

Durham House
921 Heights Blvd.
Houston, TX 77008
(713) 868-4654

Rooms: 5

The room named Heart's Desire is only one of the reasons to stop here for the night. A good innkeeper and fine cook are the other reasons.

Fairville Inn
PO Box 219
Mendenhall, PA 19357
(215) 388-5900

Rooms: 15

The inn has its own spot on a country road that leads into the city of Wilmington, Delaware. The bed-and-breakfast has charming cottage rooms and a small, inviting dining room.

Graham's B&B
150 Circle Canyon Drive
Sedona, Arizona 86336
(520) 284-1425

Rooms: 6

Don't miss the view of Sedona's red rocks from the inn's hot tub!

Hillsboro House
1933 20th Avenue South
Nashville, TN 37202
(615) 292-5501

Rooms: 3

A sleigh bed in The Magnolia Suite will have you waxing poetic, as if you've entered a Currier and Ives illustration. Next day, browse through the local historic village and listen to the chime of the carillon.

Inn at 410
410 North Leroy St.
Flagstaff, AZ 86001
(602) 774-0088

Rooms: 8

The incredible red rocks of Oak Creek Canyon set a romantic mood that is complemented back at the inn by the antiques and themed decor of this 1907 Craftsman-style home.

Inn at Olde New Berlin
321 Market Street
New Berlin, PA 17855
(717) 966-0321

Rooms: 5

The inn is a Victorian masterpiece set on the main street of a wonderfully historic village—a great spot for a walking tour.

Inn at Vaucluse Spring
140 Vaucluse Spring Lane
Stephens City, VA 22655
(540) 869-0200

Rooms: 6

Guest rooms are in three separate and historic dwellings built by artist John Chumley, including the Chumley homeplace, the guesthouse gallery, and the millhouse that was the artist's studio—a most distinctive little country inn.

Jarrett Farm Country Inn
Route 1, P.O. Box 1480
Ramona, OK 74061
(918) 371-9868

Rooms: 5

"Incredible Inndulgences" is how the
Agnew family describes its dinner at this
discriminating, sophisticated country inn
just outside Tulsa. Quail race the grounds
here. You know it's special.

King's Cottage
1049 East King Street
Lancaster, PA 17602
(717) 397-1017

Rooms: 9

The carriage house suite is "to die for."

The Lodge on Lake Lure
Route 1, Box 529A
Lake Lure, NC 28691
(704) 625-2789

Rooms: 11

You'll find a cheerful, designer lodge
atmosphere here plus incredible views of a
very special Blue Ridge Mountain lake.

Lord Mayor's Inn
435 Cedar Avenue
Long Beach, CA 90802
(310) 436-0324

Rooms: 5

The delightfully restored Edwardian
home of Long Beach's first mayor is filled
with the old and the new.

Maplewood Inn
Route 22 A South
Fair Haven, VT 05743
(802) 265-8039

Rooms: 5

Tuck yourself into a canopy, brass, or four-poster bed in this 1843 Greek Revival house. Fair Haven is one of those sleepy Vermont towns with its own village green—the perfect place to watch the stars at night.

Mercersburg Inn
405 South Main Street
Mercersburg, PA 17236
(717) 328-5231

Rooms: 15

This 20,000-square-foot manor-turned-inn dates from 1909. It has been called the largest private home ever built in the state.

Ogé House
209 Washington Street
San Antonio, TX 78204
(210) 223-2353

Rooms: 9

Located on the enchanting and famous Riverwalk, this quiet, elegant inn does its state proud. Breakfast is full and delicious.

Oliver Loud's Canal House Inn
1474 Marsh Road
Pittsford, NY 14534
(716) 248-5200

Rooms: 8

This 1810 stagecoach inn is reportedly the only historic canal house on the Erie Canal that is open to overnight guests.

Prospect Hill
Route 3, Box 430
Trevilians, VA 23093
(540) 967-0844

Rooms: 13

    Lodgings at this 1732 inn are in the elegant manor house or in a variety of charming outbuildings that were once the quarters for plantation workers. Dinner here is extra special.

Rabbit Hill Inn
Lower Waterford, VT 05848
(802) 748-5168

Rooms: 20

    There's no need for a street address here because Lower Waterford consists of one road with fewer than a dozen houses, the inn and a couple of town buildings on it. And once you arrive, you won't want to leave this quintessentially romantic New England inn and village.

Ravenwood Castle
Rt. 1, Box 52-B
New Plymouth, OH 45654
(614) 596-2606

Rooms: 10

    Incredible, brand-new Medieval castle with modern amenities. Food is delicious and rooms are grand. Service is royal.

Run of the River
9308 East Leavenworth Road
Leavenworth, WA 98826
(509) 548-7171

Rooms: 9

    The towering Cascade Mountains, a creek, and impressionistic gardens burst into view from every corner of this log-style inn that celebrates life in its food, furnishing, environment, and attitude. Lofts, wood stoves, wetlands make this place magical.

Sea Crest by the Sea
19 Tuttle Ave.
Spring Lake, NJ 07762
(908) 449-9031

Rooms: 12

    The atmosphere of a turn-of-the-century seaside holiday surrounds guests at this popular shore bed-and-breakfast. The lovely home is filled with fireplaces, featherbeds, and fantasies not to mention good cooking.

Seven Sisters Inn
820 Southeast Fort King Street
Ocala, FL 34471
(904) 867-1170

Rooms: 7

    Sip raspberry tea on the veranda, enjoy flowering walkways, or play croquet on the lawn at this meticulously restored 1888 Queen Anne Victorian in the heart of Ocala's historic district.

Squire Tarbox Inn
RR 2, Box 620
Wiscasset, ME 04578
(207) 882-7693

Rooms: 11

    The original floors, carvings, beams, moldings, and fireplaces have been preserved in the main house, which was built by Squire Samuel Tarbox in 1825. One of America's most romantic places, including the love and serenity of raising Nubian goats for the cheese here.

Tranquil House
P.O. Box 2045
Manteo, NC 27954
(919) 473-1404

Rooms: 25

    Just as its name implies, the setting is indeed peaceful in this part of North Carolina's famous Outer Banks. Family-owned, the inn strives for quality in the dining room and beyond.

Victorian Oaks
435 Locust
Minonk, IL 61760
(309) 432-2771

Rooms: 7

    Guests often congregate in the inn's parlor where they can play the organ, watch a movie, or simply get cozy by the fire.

Washington House Inn
W62 N573 Washington Ave.
Cedarburg, WI 53012
(414) 375-3550

Rooms: 29

    Breakfast is served under white pressed-tin ceilings in a room that boasts schoolhouse-style windows, and you'll love the rooms in the old chocolate factory.

The Winchester Country Inn
35 South Second St.
Ashland, OR 97520
(503) 488-1113

Rooms: 18

    Tiered gardens and gourmet dinners welcome guests at this century-old Victorian home in the heart of the cultural city of Ashland.

The Woods House
333 N. Main Street
Ashland, OR 97520
(503) 488-1598

Rooms: 6

    With names like Cupid's Chamber and the Monet Room, it is not hard to see that romance is this inn's second name. For instance, the description of the Bouquet Room begins, "A skylight brings the romance of the moon and stars to . . ."

Index